THE
EVERYTHING®
VEGAN PALEO
COOKBOOK

Dear Reader,

While it may seem like a crazy endeavor, you've just started an adventure of epic proportions. Uniting the vegan and Paleo worlds is similar to marrying fire and water. It's almost like they cancel each other out. However, I prefer to think veganism and Paleoism are more like oil and vinegar, two very different substances that, when combined, make a delicious dressing (something that will be very handy in this diet!). But just as you must vigorously shake the bottle of oil and vinegar to achieve the proper mix, the Vegan Paleo diet takes some work. It's no longer possible to grab a quick bite at the big-name fast-food joint, and gone are the days of preparing a meal straight from the preservative-filled box. This diet is all about fresh food. Food that comes from the earth and allows our bodies to thrive at the highest level. And that's what it's all about: wellness achieved through a healthy diet.

Daelyn Fortney

Welcome to the EVERYTHING® Series!

These handy, accessible books give you all you need to tackle a difficult project, gain a new hobby, comprehend a fascinating topic, prepare for an exam, or even brush up on something you learned back in school but have since forgotten.

You can choose to read an Everything® book from cover to cover or just pick out the information you want from our four useful boxes: e-questions, e-facts, e-alerts, and e-ssentials.

We give you everything you need to know on the subject, but throw in a lot of fun stuff along the way, too.

We now have more than 400 Everything® books in print, spanning such wide-ranging categories as weddings, pregnancy, cooking, music instruction, foreign language, crafts, pets, New Age, and so much more. When you're done reading them all, you can finally say you know Everything®!

QUESTION

Answers to
common questions

FACT

Important snippets
of information

ALERT

Urgent
warnings

ESSENTIAL

Quick
handy tips

PUBLISHER Karen Cooper

MANAGING EDITOR, EVERYTHING® SERIES Lisa Laing

COPY CHIEF Casey Ebert

ASSISTANT PRODUCTION EDITOR Alex Guarco

ACQUISITIONS EDITOR Lisa Laing

ASSOCIATE DEVELOPMENT EDITOR Eileen Mullan

EVERYTHING® SERIES COVER DESIGNER Erin Alexander

Visit the entire Everything® series at *www.everything.com*

THE
EVERYTHING®
VEGAN PALEO
COOKBOOK

Daelyn Fortney

Adamsmedia

Avon, Massachusetts

To Eric, Julia, Bo, and Catherine. May we always
enjoy this wild ride together.

Published by
Adams Media, a division of F+W Media, Inc.
57 Littlefield Street, Avon, MA 02322. U.S.A.
www.adamsmedia.com

Contains material adapted from *The Big Book of Paleo Recipes* by Linda Larsen, copyright © 2015 by F+W Media, Inc., ISBN 10: 1-4405-8629-2, ISBN 13: 978-1-4405-8629-3; *The Everything® Eating Clean Cookbook* by Britt Brandon, copyright © 2012 by F+W Media, Inc., ISBN 10: 1-4405-2999-X, ISBN 13: 978-1-4405-2999-3; *The Everything® Green Smoothies Book* by Britt Brandon with Lorena Novak Bull, copyright © 2011 by F+W Media, Inc., ISBN 10: 1-4405-2564-1, ISBN 13: 978-1-4405-2564-3; *The Everything® Guide to Being Vegetarian* by Alexandra Greeley, copyright © 2009 by F+W Media, Inc., ISBN 10: 1-60550-051-8, ISBN 13: 978-1-60550-051-5; *The Everything® Paleolithic Diet Book* by Jodie Cohen and Gilaad Cohen, copyright © 2011 by F+W Media, Inc., ISBN 10: 1-4405-1206-X, ISBN 13: 978-1-4405-1206-3; *The Everything® Paleolithic Diet Slow Cooker Cookbook* by Emily Dionne, copyright © 2013 by F+W Media, Inc., ISBN 10: 1-4405-5536-2, ISBN 13: 978-1-4405-5536-7; *The Everything® Vegan Cookbook* by Jolinda Hackett with Lorena Novak Bull, copyright © 2010 by F+W Media, Inc., ISBN 10: 1-4405-0216-1, ISBN 13: 978-1-4405-0216-3.

ISBN 10: 1-4405-9022-2
ISBN 13: 978-1-4405-9022-1
eISBN 10: 1-4405-9023-0
eISBN 13: 978-1-4405-9023-8

Printed in the United States of America.

10 9 8 7 6 5 4 3 2 1

Library of Congress Cataloging-in-Publication Data

Fortney, Daelyn.
  The everything vegan paleo cookbook /
Daelyn Fortney.
    pages cm
  Includes index.
  ISBN 978-1-4405-9022-1 (pb) -- ISBN 1-4405-9022-2
(pb) -- ISBN 978-1-4405-9023-8 (ebook) -- ISBN 1-4405-
9023-0 (ebook)
  1. Vegan cooking. 2. Prehistoric peoples--
Nutrition. I. Title.
  TX837.F658 2015
  641.5'636--dc23
                    2015010414

Contents

Acknowledgments

I wish to thank my family for their unwavering love and support, my friends for their endless interest in my endeavors, and my readers for allowing me to be part of their journeys.

Introduction

IMAGINE TAKING TWO VERY different diets and combining them into one unique super way of eating. Enter the Vegan Paleo diet. On the surface, the vegan and Paleo plans are quite opposite. Adopting a vegan diet means cutting out all animal products and achieving protein requirements through grains and legumes. The Paleo diet focuses only on foods that cavemen thrived on, and much of the protein comes from meats and fish. So how can the Vegan Paleo diet really work?

Rather than letting the differences become obstacles, it's best to spotlight the similarities in the vegan and Paleo worlds. Both diets celebrate natural food items like fruits, vegetables, nuts, and seeds. By allowing these gifts from nature to be the focal point, the vegan diet and Paleo diet can be joined, creating a wholesome and satisfying union. Additionally, the health benefits of both regimens separately are undeniable, and, with mindful melding, the two together create a superstar diet that is beneficial to the body, mind, and soul.

Whether you've been practicing the Vegan Paleo diet for years or you are simply curious and looking to try something new, it's important to have support during your journey. That's precisely what this book is designed to do—offer you the tools needed to help make food choices that are right for you and your lifestyle.

Of course, learning the ins and outs of the diets separately is the perfect place to start. It's important to understand what the vegan and Paleo diets entail and why they are practiced. Once you do that, it will be easier to grasp how the two can be joined. As you learn how to incorporate foods common to both diets, eliminating those that don't fit with one or the other and allowing the two to nutritionally complement each other, you'll realize that the Vegan Paleo diet is a completely achievable venture. Then it's on to the cooking!

With such an extreme pairing of diets, it's easy to overthink what you can and can't eat. This book will guide you by offering an extensive selection of culinary delights spanning from breakfast to lunch to dinner and everything in between. All the dishes are delicious, nutritious, and perfectly pair the vegan and Paleo diets. By developing a deeper appreciation of the foods presented by Mother Nature herself, you'll see how you can take your meals to a new level. You'll learn how to make meals that not only please you, but will impress even the most hardcore modern-day eater.

When moving through the Vegan Paleo adventure, you'll be amazed by the enticing fare that can be created with such pure ingredients: mouthwatering Ratatouille, sweet and savory salads, decadent spreads, and refreshing sorbets. However, every new diet should be viewed as an exploration of sorts, a search for a new food identity that allows you to reach your goals, whatever they might be. It's imperative to remember that no one is perfect, and your expectations should reflect this. Take your time as you learn how to cook with these united diets. Enjoy the process. Taste the flavors. Tap into the good health that your body wants, needs, and deserves.

CHAPTER 1

Combining the Vegan and Paleo Diets Into One Healthy Plan

The vegan diet is known to have extensive health benefits, and the same can be said for the Paleo diet. Imagine what could happen if the two were combined into one unique plan in which fresh, real foods are the superstars of each meal. The Vegan Paleo diet does just that, treating the body as a temple by only allowing consumption of plant-based foods found in nature. The diet is a healthful option if you're looking to change your life by making more conscious food decisions.

The Vegan Diet

The vegan diet avoids the consumption of all animal-derived products, including dairy and eggs. *Vegan*, by definition, is a word used to explain a complete lifestyle, one that is lived in a manner that avoids as much harm to sentient beings as possible. Ethical vegans not only shun all animal products in food; they also eliminate use of animal-sourced items in their overall day-to-day lives. Products deriving from animals or exploiting creatures in some manner, including leather, wool, silk, pearls, and beeswax, do not fit into the vegan lifestyle.

Ethical vegans have long touted the health benefits received from eating only plant-based foods. A well-planned vegan diet is high in fiber and low in saturated fat, and incorporates above-average consumption of fruits and vegetables. Additionally, cholesterol is not consumed in any amount.

Cholesterol, a sterol that is produced by the liver and occurs in all cells of the body, is found in all animal products. Although the waxy substance is essential for life, the body produces all it needs to function properly. Consuming too much cholesterol can be dangerous, as it leads to plaque formation between the layers of the artery walls, making the heart work harder to circulate blood. Studies show that vegans have a lower risk of some of today's biggest health issues, including type 2 diabetes, cardiovascular disease, obesity, and some forms of cancer, possibly due to the absence of cholesterol in the diet.

ESSENTIAL

Remember, animal products are found in many common sauces and dressings. For example, traditional pesto sauce is made with Parmesan cheese, and Caesar salad dressing typically contains anchovy fillets.

Today's health-conscious world noticed these benefits, and as a result veganism has taken on a new form: the vegan for health reasons. Those opting for a plant-based diet typically follow the same dietary guidelines (no meat, no dairy, no eggs, no animal-derived ingredients), but improving their health and decreasing their chance of disease is their motivating factor.

What Can a Vegan Eat?

Contrary to popular belief, vegans can fill their refrigerators and pantries with a vast assortment of foods. Pasta, soup, tortillas, cereal, bagels, potato chips, and crackers are just some of the "normal" products vegans can consume. Additionally, more and more companies are producing vegan-friendly products.

Determining whether an item is vegan is actually quite simple. Ask yourself, "Did this come from a living creature?" If the answer is "Yes," then it isn't vegan.

- **What about seafood?** Does seafood come from a living creature? Fish, lobsters, and shrimp are all living creatures; therefore, seafood is not vegan.
- **What about honey?** Does honey come from a living creature? Honey is made by honeybees, which are living creatures; therefore, honey is not vegan.
- **What about gelatin?** Does gelatin come from a living creature? Gelatin is obtained through the boiling of bones, ligaments, and skin of animals; therefore, gelatin is not vegan.

In short, anything that is derived from an animal is off-limits in the vegan diet.

Of course, it's easy to know not to consume a hamburger, macaroni and cheese, or an omelet, and it's just as easy to know that salads, spaghetti with marinara, and tofu over rice are all on the "Yes" list, but things get tricky when trying to indulge in convenient foods—boxed, canned, and prepackaged meals. Reading food labels is imperative when practicing a vegan lifestyle. However, in reality, even those who do not have dietary restrictions should adopt the habit of reading labels. It's important to know what's going into your body.

ALERT

When reading labels, look for "hidden" animal ingredients. For example, cochineal extract, also called carmine, is used as a dye in certain foods. The bright red additive is made from crushed cochineal insects (scale insects). This is not a vegan-friendly ingredient.

Where Do Vegans Get Protein?

The most frequent question vegans receive is "Where do you get your protein?" The answer is "everywhere." Protein is found in numerous plant-based sources as well as in meat and animal products. Nearly all natural foods (fruits, vegetables, grains, beans, nuts, and seeds) contain some amount of protein.

Plant-based protein sources include lentils, couscous, tofu, tempeh, quinoa, peanuts, sunflower seeds, oatmeal, almonds, whole-wheat bread, black beans, chickpeas, corn, peas, avocado, spinach, flaxseed, broccoli, brown rice, seitan, edamame, great northern beans, chia seeds, and artichokes.

The Paleo Diet

The Paleo diet celebrates the foods that were consumed during the Paleolithic era, also called the Old Stone Age—a time period that extended from the beginning of human existence (2.5 million years ago) until approximately 12,000 B.C.E. Paleolithic people were hunter-gatherers whose diet consisted only of items found in nature—meats, poultry, fish, insects, eggs, leafy greens, fruits, berries, nuts, and seeds.

ESSENTIAL

Paleolithic hunter-gatherers ate foods that were pre-agricultural. They did not farm the land or herd animals for sustenance. Grains such as wheat, oats, barley, quinoa, and rice were not a part of their diet. White potatoes and legumes, such as soybeans and peanuts, also were not available.

Today's Paleo embraces the same pre-agricultural diet as that of his ancient ancestors. The Paleo diet is filled with foods that would have been hunted and gathered by cavemen. Of course, in today's modern society, those consuming a Paleo diet need not head to the forest, fields, and streams to find their food. It's simply a matter of understanding the dos and don'ts of primitive foods.

FACT

Fifty percent of the ancient diet of the Paleolithic era was composed of fruits and vegetables, compared to a mere 10–15 percent of the modern diet. Ironically, all the fresh produce you desire is just miles away at the nearest grocery store. Your Old Stone Age ancestors handpicked their own.

The Paleo diet has become increasingly popular with people looking to live a healthier lifestyle. Because processed foods and refined sugars are shunned and dairy and carbs are eliminated, the diet is used to develop a lean yet muscular body composition. Additionally, it is believed that the Paleo lifestyle has many health benefits, including increased energy levels and reduced risk of diseases such as diabetes, heart disease, obesity, and cancer.

What Can a Paleo Eat?

Paleo people lived off the land, and everything they ate was natural. Living a very simplistic lifestyle by necessity, they hunted and gathered their foods and cooked them over a fire.

To determine whether an item is Paleo, you must simply decide whether a caveman could have consumed the product. Fresh meats, fresh vegetables, and fresh fruits take center stage in today's Paleo diet. The key is keeping it simple and consuming only foods that come straight from the earth, neither processed nor artificial in any way.

ESSENTIAL

Oils used in a Paleo diet include olive oil, coconut oil, flaxseed oil, avocado oil, walnut oil, and animal fat. Canola oil, peanut oil, corn oil, and soybean oil are to be avoided.

Foods that should be avoided when practicing the Paleo lifestyle include anything containing artificial ingredients as well as dairy, grains, legumes, and potatoes. No milk or cheese. No breads or bagels. No beans, peanuts, peas, or soy. Additionally, participating in the Paleo diet means no refined sugars and no refined vegetable oils.

Where Do Paleos Get Protein?

It is easy to see where people following the Paleo diet get their protein: animal sources. Meat plays a large role in the Paleo lifestyle. Ideally Paleo meats are either organic and grass-fed or wild game. Although meats make up a large portion of the diet, it is recommended that you steer clear of meats high in fat; lean meats are preferable. Fish, seafood, poultry, and eggs are also acceptable.

Vegan Meets Paleo

To optimize the health benefits of both the vegan diet and Paleo diet, many people have turned to the unique Vegan Paleo diet. However, combining the vegan and Paleo worlds is quite an undertaking. The vegan diet relies heavily on legumes and grains for protein, and these items are avoided when practicing the Paleo diet. The Paleo diet relies heavily on animal products (eggs, meat, poultry, and fish) for protein. Without exception, animal products are not included in the vegan diet. Simply put, typical sources of protein cannot be crossed over.

To marry the two diets and still fulfill the recommended daily protein requirements means focusing meals around two common protein sources: nuts and seeds. And the melding of the diets includes taking advantage of other commonalities: leafy greens, vegetables, and fruits.

FACT

It is recommended that adult men and women receive 10–35 percent of their daily calories from protein. That amounts to about 46 grams of protein for women and 56 grams for men. One cup of almonds contains 20 grams of protein. One cup of sunflower seeds contains 29 grams of protein.

While the focus of the union seems limiting—who wants to eat almonds and sunflower seeds for dinner?—it's actually quite possible to make delicious fare with the minimal allowable ingredients. Rather than picturing a plate full of vegetables and nuts, imagine what you can do with those items. Raw cashews can be turned into a delicious vegan- and Paleo-friendly garlic Alfredo sauce (see recipe for Cashew Alfredo Sauce in Chapter 12). That sauce can be used to coat grilled eggplant. Or toss the sauce with spaghetti squash for a unique twist on pasta. It's all about thinking outside the box . . . literally.

FACT

A member of the same family as broccoli and cauliflower, kale is a superfood packed with essential nutrients for a healthy body, including beta carotene, calcium, iron, and magnesium as well as vitamins A, C, and K.

Besides taking advantage of nature's bounty, those who have already chosen a vegan lifestyle will also benefit from the lack of artificial and processed foods in the Paleo diet. There will no longer be a need to read boxes or canned labels, because with the infusion of the Paleo diet, those items are virtually eliminated. It's all about whole foods.

Additionally, junk foods and refined vegetable oils are on the "No" list in the Paleo world, and therefore not allowed in the Vegan Paleo diet. Junk foods can be replaced with healthy alternatives including kale or sweet potato chips, and olive or coconut oil is an ideal substitute for refined vegetable oils.

Vegan Paleo Sweeteners

Following any type of plan with a dietary restriction can be challenging, and, when merging the vegan and Paleo diets, things get especially tricky. Not only do the diets focus on opposite protein sources; additional conflicts exist, sweeteners being one of them. Raw honey is a popular sweetener among Paleos and is often used to add sweetness to smoothies and desserts. Obviously, the bee-produced substance is not vegan-friendly, which makes it a "No" in the Vegan Paleo diet. While most sweeteners are processed in some manner, three alternatives to honey are generally accepted in the Paleo world: maple syrup, stevia, and coconut sugar. However, it's important to note that following a strict Paleo diet means choosing sweeteners with a low glycemic load (GL) and using those sweeteners sparingly.

The term *glycemic load* refers to a measurement used to determine how much a consumed food will raise the body's blood glucose. GL is calculated by multiplying the food's glycemic index (GI) number by the carbohydrates in a serving. Paleos choose to consume items with low glycemic loads because the lower value has less impact on the body's blood sugar levels. By keeping the levels more consistent and avoiding sharp rises, a low-glycemic diet helps stabilize the body's weight and, in turn, prevents obesity-related diseases. Low GI foods are also connected to improved moods and increased energy.

The Part-Time Vegan Paleo

When studied separately, both the vegan diet and the Paleo diet have been shown to reduce the chances of certain diseases. No doubt, when combined, the resulting Vegan Paleo diet has extensive health benefits. Even so, it may be difficult to follow a strict Vegan Paleo diet on a full-time basis.

With that in mind, there is no harm in choosing one diet as your main lifestyle and incorporating meals that meet the requirements of both. Think of it as a Vegan Paleo challenge of sorts. Start with at least one meal a day that includes foods that adhere to the union. Choosing to be a part-time Vegan Paleo may also help with obstacles such as those faced by the vegan who doesn't want to permanently give up legumes and grains and the Paleo who prefers to keep meat on the menu.

Vegan Paleo Shopping

The Vegan Paleo diet is all about harnessing the power of nature. This makes shopping trips pretty simple. Your main focus is the produce section, with quick stops in the spice, nut, and frozen food (vegetables and fruits) aisles.

ESSENTIAL

It's okay to choose frozen fruits and veggies. In fact, the frozen food section is a great place to check for your favorite produce during the off-season.

Some people argue that the vegan and Paleo diets are expensive. This is an unfortunate view because, as with any diet, it's all about how someone chooses to shop. It's very possible to practice each of the diets while adhering to a strict budget. Of course combining the two removes some of the perceived expenses, like pricier grains and premium cuts of meat. But there are still certain items that can be more expensive than the traditional counterparts. For example, coconut sugar is more expensive than white sugar, and a bag of almonds is most certainly more expensive than a bag of potato chips. Still, the crux of the combined diet is vegetables. As far as bang for your buck is concerned, it doesn't get better than the items located in the produce section.

Consider locating a farmers' market or produce co-op. Both celebrate the "farm to fork" mentality by offering locally grown foods. And often you can leave with a full bag of groceries for a fraction of what it would cost at your neighborhood supermarket.

Getting Started

Ready to dive into the Vegan Paleo diet? Before you get started, there are some important notes to remember.

Understand that to get the most out of any diet, it's imperative to embrace the plan as a complete lifestyle change. This diet is not just about what you can and can't eat; it's about living for longevity by making more calculated food choices.

Additionally, as with any diet or lifestyle change, you don't have to be perfect. Much can be said for the health benefits of keeping one's sanity. Therefore, if you find you are having a difficult time sticking with the plan, incorporate foods that help ease the stress. Find a comfort zone that works for you and your day-to-day life.

Consider keeping a journal to document your experiences. And look for support. Reach out to others who have an understanding of the diets, whether separate or combined.

Finally, have fun with the diet. By going on the Vegan Paleo adventure, you are looking at your food from a different perspective. Not many people have chosen to be part of such an elite club. As such, you should be proud of your journey.

CHAPTER 2

Breakfast

Toasted Nut "Cereal"

Cereal is an easy weekday breakfast. But packaged products are loaded with sweeteners, preservatives, and artificial colors. Make your own "cereal" and you won't miss the packaged stuff at all.

INGREDIENTS | MAKES 10 CUPS

1½ cups pumpkin seeds
1 cup sunflower seeds
1½ cups sliced almonds
1½ cups chopped pecans
1½ cups unsweetened shredded coconut
⅓ cup maple syrup
⅓ cup coconut oil
1 teaspoon cinnamon
2 teaspoons vanilla
1 cup dried cranberries
1 cup chopped dried apricots
1 cup golden raisins

1. Preheat oven to 375°F. Line a rimmed baking sheet with parchment paper and set aside.

2. In a large bowl, combine pumpkin seeds, sunflower seeds, almonds, pecans, and coconut. Pour mixture onto lined baking sheet.

3. In a small saucepan, combine maple syrup and coconut oil and heat gently until coconut oil is melted. Remove from heat and stir in cinnamon and vanilla. Drizzle over the mixture on baking sheet and toss to coat. Spread evenly.

4. Bake for 20–30 minutes, stirring every 10 minutes, until light golden brown and fragrant. Remove from oven and stir in cranberries, apricots, and raisins. Let stand until cool, stirring occasionally. Store in an airtight container at room temperature.

Coconut Muesli

Muesli is typically a mixture of raw oats, seeds, nuts, and dried fruits. But here's a surprise: You don't need the oatmeal! Coconut flakes make an admirable substitute. Plus, they're flavorful and filled with fiber and healthy fat.

INGREDIENTS | SERVES 8

2 cups unsweetened coconut flakes
2 cups slivered almonds
1 cup chopped macadamia nuts
1 cup broken walnuts
½ cup sesame seeds
½ cup pumpkin seeds
1 cup golden raisins
1 cup dried unsweetened cranberries
1 cup chopped Medjool dates
1 teaspoon cinnamon
1 teaspoon ground ginger
½ teaspoon nutmeg
8 cups almond or hazelnut milk

1. In a large bowl, combine all ingredients except milk and mix well. Store in an airtight container at room temperature.

2. To serve, pour 1 cup muesli into a bowl and add 1 cup almond or hazelnut milk. Let stand for 5 minutes before eating.

3. You can also make this muesli the night before. Place muesli in a large bowl and cover with milk or water. Cover and let stand overnight in the refrigerator. When you're ready to eat breakfast, stir the muesli and dig in.

Crunchy Muesli

For a crunchier muesli, toast the coconut flakes, nuts, and seeds. Spread on a baking sheet and bake at 350°F for 10–15 minutes until fragrant and light brown. Cool before combining with remaining ingredients.

Nutty Granola

Granola is usually made with oatmeal, which is a no-no on the Paleo plan. But there are enough different types of nuts and seeds, together with coconut, to make an admirable granola with no grains. Using raw nuts adds to the authenticity of the recipe. But if you can't find them, use roasted nuts; just cut the time in the oven by half.

INGREDIENTS | MAKES 10 CUPS

1 cup raw almonds
1 cup raw pecan pieces
1 cup raw hazelnuts
1 cup raw pumpkin seeds
1 cup shelled raw sunflower seeds
2 cups unsweetened coconut flakes
1 cup unsweetened grated coconut
½ cup maple syrup
½ cup coconut oil
2 teaspoons cinnamon
1 teaspoon nutmeg
½ teaspoon salt
1 cup golden raisins or dried blueberries
1 cup dried unsweetened cherries

1. Preheat oven to 325°F. Place ¼ cup each almonds, pecans, hazelnuts, and pumpkin seeds in a blender or food processor. Blend or process until finely chopped.

2. Combine finely chopped nuts with remaining almonds, pecans, hazelnuts, and pumpkin seeds in a large bowl. Stir in sunflower seeds, coconut flakes, and grated coconut.

3. In a small saucepan, combine maple syrup and coconut oil and heat just until oil melts. Stir in cinnamon, nutmeg, and salt.

4. Pour the maple syrup mixture over the nut and seed mixture. Stir well.

5. Spread granola mixture on a large (15" × 10") rimmed baking sheet. Bake for about 30 minutes, stirring every 10 minutes, until mixture is golden brown. Let cool completely, and then stir in raisins (or blueberries) and cherries. Store in an airtight container at room temperature for up to a few weeks.

Dried Fruit Porridge

This fruit- and nut-studded hot cereal is loaded with fiber, vitamin E, and omega-3 fatty acids. It's wonderful with almond or coconut milk.

INGREDIENTS | SERVES 6

½ cup raisins or dried cranberries
¼ cup slivered almonds
¼ cup raw pumpkin seeds
¼ cup raw sunflower seeds
¼ cup unsweetened shredded coconut
⅛ cup maple syrup
2 tablespoons coconut butter, melted

1. Line a baking sheet with parchment paper and set aside.

2. Place raisins (or dried cranberries), almonds, pumpkin seeds, sunflower seeds, and coconut in a 4-quart slow cooker. Add maple syrup and coconut butter and toss to coat.

3. Cover (but vent with a chopstick) and cook on high for 2½–3½ hours, stirring periodically to prevent burning.

4. Cool porridge by spreading it out in a single layer on lined baking sheet.

Soft Breakfast Bread

Using a combination of puréed fruits and vegetables will make a more interesting final product. This bread is delicious served as-is for breakfast, or try it as a substitute for ordinary bread in your favorite French toast recipe.

INGREDIENTS | MAKES 1 LOAF

½ cup solid-pack pumpkin

½ cup puréed canned pears

3 teaspoons Ener-G Egg Replacer mixed with 4 tablespoons water

¾ cup maple syrup

¼ cup coconut milk

1 teaspoon vanilla

1 cup almond flour

¾ cup coconut flour

2 tablespoons arrowroot powder

½ teaspoon salt

⅛ teaspoon baking soda

¼ teaspoon cream of tartar

½ teaspoon cinnamon

¼ teaspoon nutmeg

¼ teaspoon cardamom

1. Preheat oven to 350°F. Line a 9" × 5" loaf pan with parchment paper and set aside.

2. In a large bowl, combine pumpkin, pears, egg replacer, maple syrup, coconut milk, and vanilla and beat well.

3. In a medium bowl, stir together almond flour, coconut flour, arrowroot powder, salt, baking soda, cream of tartar, cinnamon, nutmeg, and cardamom.

4. Add the dry ingredients to the pumpkin mixture and mix well. Pour into prepared loaf pan.

5. Bake for 40–50 minutes or until a toothpick inserted in the center comes out clean. Cool in pan for 15 minutes, then remove loaf and move to a wire rack to cool completely.

Vanilla-Flavored Poached Autumn Fruits

Enjoy as breakfast or as dessert for a sweet end to a hearty meal.

INGREDIENTS | SERVES 5

2 medium Granny Smith apples, peeled, cored, and halved (save cores)

2 medium Bartlett pears, peeled, cored, and halved (save cores)

1 large orange, peeled, seeded, and halved

⅔ cup maple syrup

1 vanilla bean, split and seeded (save seeds)

1 cinnamon stick

1. Place apple and pear cores in a 4½-quart slow cooker.

2. Squeeze juice from orange halves into the slow cooker and add orange halves, maple syrup, vanilla bean and seeds, and cinnamon stick.

3. Add apples and pears and pour in enough water to cover the fruit. Stir, cover, and cook on high for 2–3 hours, until fruit is tender.

4. Remove apple and pear halves and set aside. Strain cooking liquids into a large saucepan and simmer gently over low heat until liquid reduces by half and thickens. Discard solids.

5. Dice apples and pears and add to saucepan to warm.

6. To serve, spoon fruit with sauce into bowls.

Nuts and Seeds Granola Bars

Most commercial granola bars are loaded with sugar and artificial ingredients. Make your own healthy granola bars for a satisfying snack. You can vary the nuts and fruits in these bars as you like.

INGREDIENTS | MAKES 24 BARS

1½ cups slivered almonds
1½ cups sunflower seeds
1 cup chopped pecans
1½ cups unsweetened shredded coconut
1 cup dried unsweetened cherries
½ cup maple syrup
⅔ cup almond butter
2 teaspoons vanilla
1 teaspoon cinnamon
¼ teaspoon nutmeg
½ teaspoon salt

1. Preheat oven to 350°F. Line a 9" × 13" rimmed baking pan with parchment paper and set aside.

2. Place ¾ cup almonds, ¾ cup sunflower seeds, and ½ cup pecans in a food processor and process until finely chopped.

3. In a large bowl, combine chopped seeds and nuts with remaining almonds, sunflower seeds, and pecans. Stir in coconut and cherries.

4. In a small saucepan over medium heat, bring maple syrup to a simmer. Simmer for 1 minute, then pour over nut mixture. Add almond butter, vanilla, cinnamon, nutmeg, and salt and mix until well combined.

5. Place in prepared pan and press down firmly with hands greased with coconut oil or more parchment paper until evenly distributed.

6. Bake for 20–30 minutes or until bars are light golden brown. Cool completely, then refrigerate overnight. Cut into bars to serve.

Old-Fashioned Sweet Potato Hash Browns

These sweet potato hash browns are likely to become a family favorite. They are easy to make and packed with Paleo and vegan flavor your entire family will love.

INGREDIENTS | SERVES 6

3 tablespoons coconut oil

3 medium sweet potatoes, peeled and grated

1 tablespoon cinnamon

1. Heat coconut oil in a large skillet over medium-high heat. Cook sweet potatoes in hot oil for 7 minutes, stirring often. Drain on paper towels.

2. Sprinkle sweet potatoes with cinnamon and serve.

Chai Tea

Store any leftover tea in a covered container in the refrigerator. It can be reheated, but leftover tea is best served over ice.

INGREDIENTS | SERVES 12

5 cups water
6 slices fresh ginger
1 teaspoon whole cloves
2 (3") cinnamon sticks
1½ teaspoons freshly ground nutmeg
½ teaspoon ground cardamom
1 cup maple syrup
12 bags black tea
6 cups coconut milk

Sweet Tip

If you prefer, you can omit adding the maple syrup during the cooking process and allow each drinker to sweeten his or her serving according to taste.

1. Pour water into a 4-quart slow cooker. Put ginger and cloves in a muslin spice bag or a piece of cheesecloth secured with a piece of kitchen twine; add to the cooker along with cinnamon sticks, nutmeg, and cardamom. Cover and cook on low for 4–6 hours or on high for 2–3 hours.

2. Stir in maple syrup until it's dissolved into the water. Add tea bags and coconut milk; cover and cook on low for 30 minutes. Remove and discard the spices in the muslin bag or cheesecloth, the cinnamon sticks, and the tea bags. Ladle into tea cups or mugs to serve.

Spiced Tea

This tea can be served hot or over ice. You can change the flavor quite easily with different varieties of herbal teas.

INGREDIENTS | SERVES 6

4 bags herbal tea
1 teaspoon ground nutmeg
½ teaspoon ground cinnamon
¼ teaspoon ground cloves
6 cups boiling water

1. In a ceramic teapot, combine tea bags and spices.

2. Pour boiling water into teapot. Steep for 5 minutes, then remove tea bags.

Berry Smoothies

Smoothies are easy to make as long as you have a good blender. Look for one with reverse action or one that is marketed as good for making crushed ice. You can vary this recipe any way you'd like, using the berries and fruits you like best. This recipe even sneaks in a tomato to add more nutrition, but it can be omitted.

INGREDIENTS | SERVES 3

1 cup sliced strawberries
1 cup raspberries
1 medium Roma tomato, seeded and chopped
1 cup coconut milk
2 tablespoons maple syrup
½ teaspoon vanilla
3 ice cubes

Combine all ingredients in a blender and blend until smooth. Pour immediately into glasses and serve.

Vanilla Date Breakfast Smoothie

Adding dates to a basic almond milk and fruit smoothie adds a blast of unexpected sweetness. It's a healthy breakfast treat or a cooling summer snack.

INGREDIENTS | SERVES 1

4 large pitted dates
Water
¾ cup almond milk
2 medium bananas, peeled
6 ice cubes
¼ teaspoon vanilla

1. In a small bowl, cover dates with water and soak for at least 10 minutes. Discard soaking water and add dates and all other ingredients to a blender.

2. Process about 1 minute on medium speed until smooth.

Apricot Banana Smoothie

Apricot and banana together make a delicious and refreshing smoothie.

INGREDIENTS | SERVES 1

3 medium apricots, pitted
1 medium banana, peeled
1 cup coconut milk
4 teaspoons maple syrup
4–6 ice cubes

Combine all ingredients in blender and blend until smooth and frosty.

Apricots Are Quite Beneficial

Apricots are often overlooked as a fruit choice, but these little tangy fruits are an excellent source of vitamins A, C, and E, potassium, and iron. You could fulfill almost 50 percent of your vitamin A daily value with three apricots a day.

Flaxseed Smoothie

This quick treat is a great snack with the powerful punch of omega-3 fatty acids. Strawberries contain high antioxidant levels to make this smoothie a perfect and refreshing snack on a hot afternoon.

INGREDIENTS | SERVES 1

½ medium banana, peeled and frozen
1 cup frozen strawberries
2 tablespoons ground flaxseed
1 cup vanilla coconut, almond, or hazelnut milk

Place all ingredients in blender. Purée until smooth.

Flaxseed

Flaxseed is a great way to introduce more omega-3 fatty acids into your diet. These little powerhouses are small, easily transported, and virtually flavorless. They can be added easily into any smoothie or salad for a little anti-inflammatory benefit.

Avocado Smoothie

This quick blended smoothie is a sweet treat when you're looking for something refreshing that resembles a milkshake.

INGREDIENTS | SERVES 1

1 large ripe avocado, pitted and peeled
1 cup coconut milk
½ cup almond milk
3 tablespoons maple syrup
3–4 ice cubes

In a blender combine all ingredients until smooth. Serve chilled.

Avocado Milkshakes

In the Philippines, Brazil, Indonesia, Vietnam, and south India, avocados are often used in milkshakes. If you are craving a delicious chocolate treat, try this recipe with added cacao nibs.

Blueberry Antioxidant Smoothie

Blueberries contain one of the highest antioxidant levels found in fruit. This refreshing smoothie fights free-radical oxidation in your body.

INGREDIENTS | SERVES 1

1 cup frozen blueberries
½ medium avocado, peeled and pitted
1 cup vanilla almond milk
⅛ teaspoon ground nutmeg
4–6 ice cubes

Combine all ingredients in a blender and purée until smooth.

Almond Joy Smoothie

This chocolate and coconut smoothie is a real treat when you are craving something sweet.

INGREDIENTS | SERVES 1

1 cup coconut milk
½ cup cacao nibs
3 tablespoons maple syrup
½ teaspoon cinnamon
¼ teaspoon nutmeg
4–6 ice cubes

Combine all ingredients in a blender and purée until smooth.

The Green Go-Getter Smoothie

Packed with spinach and green apples, this creamy smoothie will kick your morning off with a boost of essential amino acids, vitamins, minerals, and an absolutely amazing taste.

INGREDIENTS | MAKES 3–4 CUPS

1 cup spinach

2 medium green apples, peeled and cored

1 medium banana, peeled

1 cup water, divided

1. Place spinach, apples, banana, and ½ cup water in a blender and blend until thoroughly combined.

2. Continue adding remaining water while blending until desired texture is achieved.

A Smoothie for Even the Greenest Green Smoothie Maker!

Some people who are new to creating green smoothies can have a hard time enjoying the powerful taste of the greens. The combination of bananas, apples, and spinach, with more fruit than greens, provides an appetizing taste that is sweeter and lessens the intensity of the spinach. This smoothie is a great starter for anyone who is turned off by the overpowering taste of greens.

Breakfast Carrot Smoothie

Rich in beta-carotene, this smoothie blends romaine lettuce with tasty carrots and apples to give you a sweet start that can help you stay focused, provide lasting energy, and maintain healthy eyes and metabolism.

INGREDIENTS | MAKES 1 QUART

2 cups chopped romaine lettuce
3 medium carrots, peeled and chopped
1 medium apple, peeled and cored
1 cup water

1. Combine first 3 ingredients in a blender.

2. Add water slowly while blending until desired texture is achieved.

Cherry Vanilla Smoothie

Start your day with a sweet and satisfying cherry smoothie.

INGREDIENTS | SERVES 2

2 cups pitted cherries
1 medium banana, peeled
Pulp of 1 vanilla bean
1 cup vanilla almond milk
1 teaspoon vanilla extract
1 cup ice, divided

1. Combine cherries, banana, vanilla bean pulp, almond milk, and vanilla extract in the blender with ½ cup ice and blend until thoroughly combined.

2. Add remaining ice gradually while blending until desired consistency is reached.

Where to Find Vanilla Beans

Vanilla beans can be found at your local grocery store with other dried herbs and/or baking essentials. Slit the bean down the center with a sharp knife, open the skin, and reveal the pulp. This pulp is the ingredient referred to in most cookbooks.

Mango Banana Smoothie

Since mangoes are now available frozen year-round, you can try this treat any time of year.

INGREDIENTS | SERVES 2

1 cup chopped mango
1 large banana, peeled
1 cup vanilla almond milk
2 cups ice, divided

Mangoes Year-Round

If you can't find mangoes fresh out of season, look in your grocer's freezer. This vibrant fruit can be enjoyed year-round thanks to the manufacturers who have prepared, peeled, flash-frozen, and packaged this delicious treat.

1. Combine mango, banana, and almond milk in a blender with ½ cup ice and blend until thoroughly combined.

2. Add remaining ice gradually while blending until desired consistency is reached.

Tropical Paradise Smoothie

The combination of tropical fruit makes a light and satisfying smoothie
that will rejuvenate your energy and awaken your taste buds!

INGREDIENTS | SERVES 2

1½ cups mashed and softened coconut meat

1 cup chopped pineapple

½ cup chopped mango

1 medium clementine, peeled

2 cups coconut milk

2 cups ice, divided

1. Combine coconut, pineapple, mango, clementine, and coconut milk in a blender with ½ cup ice and blend until thoroughly combined.

2. Add remaining ice gradually while blending until desired consistency is reached.

Perfect Pear Smoothie

Use ripe, juicy pears for this delicious smoothie. Cinnamon rounds out the fruit flavor,
but you can also try other warm spices, like nutmeg, cloves, or cardamom.

INGREDIENTS | SERVES 2

3 medium pears, peeled, cored, and sliced

1 banana, peeled

1 cup vanilla almond milk

1 teaspoon cinnamon

2 cups ice, divided

1. Preheat oven to 375°F. Layer pears in a shallow baking dish. Add enough water to cover the bottom of the baking dish, and bake for 20–30 minutes or until pears are fork-tender.

2. Combine pears, banana, almond milk, and cinnamon in a blender with ½ cup ice and blend until thoroughly combined.

3. Add remaining ice gradually while blending until desired consistency is reached.

Pears for Fiber

In addition to being an abundant source of vitamins and minerals like vitamins B and C, folic acid, niacin, phosphorus, and calcium, pears are a great source of fiber. A diet with adequate fiber will ensure that any gastrointestinal issues are a thing of the past.

Easy Lunches

Herb-Stuffed Tomatoes

Serve these Italian-influenced stuffed tomatoes with a simple salad for an easy, light meal.

INGREDIENTS | SERVES 2

2 large tomatoes

1 stalk celery, minced

1 tablespoon minced fresh garlic

2 tablespoons minced fresh oregano

2 tablespoons minced fresh Italian parsley

1 teaspoon dried chervil

1 teaspoon fennel seeds

¾ cup water

1. Cut out the core of each tomato and discard. Scoop the seeds out of the tomatoes, leaving the walls intact.

2. In a small bowl, stir together celery, garlic, herbs, and fennel seeds. Divide into 2 even portions, and stuff 1 portion into the center of each tomato.

3. Place filled tomatoes in a 4-quart slow cooker. Pour water into the bottom of the slow cooker. Cook on low for 4 hours.

Cold Spanish Gazpacho with Avocado

Gazpacho is best enjoyed on an outdoor patio just after sunset on a warm summer evening. But really, any time you want a simple, light starter soup will do, no matter the weather.

INGREDIENTS | SERVES 6

2 medium cucumbers, peeled and diced

½ medium red onion, peeled and diced

2 large tomatoes, diced

¼ cup chopped fresh cilantro

2 avocados, peeled, pitted, and diced

4 cloves garlic, peeled

2 tablespoons lime juice

1 tablespoon apple cider vinegar

¾ cup Basic Vegetable Stock (see recipe in Chapter 6)

1 small jalapeño pepper, seeded and chopped

1 teaspoon salt

½ teaspoon ground black pepper

1. In a large bowl, mix together cucumbers, onion, tomatoes, cilantro, and avocados. Set half of the mixture aside. Place the other half in a food processor or blender and pulse to mix. Add garlic, lime juice, vinegar, vegetable stock, and jalapeño and process until smooth.

2. Transfer mixture to the bowl with the reserved cucumbers, onion, tomatoes, cilantro, and avocados. Stir gently to combine. Season with salt and pepper.

3. Chill in the refrigerator for at least 4 hours before serving.

Simple Tomato Soup

This simple, healthy, three-step soup is made with canned tomatoes, which are available year-round at affordable prices. You can also make this soup with about 4 pounds of chopped fresh tomatoes if you prefer.

INGREDIENTS | SERVES 8

1 small sweet onion, peeled and finely diced

3 tablespoons coconut butter

3 (14.5-ounce) cans diced tomatoes

1 tablespoon maple syrup

15 ounces Roasted Vegetable Stock (see recipe in Chapter 6)

½ teaspoon lemon juice

1. In a small microwave-safe bowl cook onion and coconut butter in the microwave on high for 1 minute.

2. Grease a 4-quart slow cooker with coconut oil and place onion mixture, tomatoes, maple syrup, and stock in it. Cook on high for 4 hours or on low for 8 hours.

3. Turn off slow cooker and add lemon juice to the soup. Cool soup for about 20 minutes, then blend using an immersion blender or by pouring the soup (a little at a time) into a kitchen blender.

Paleo Sandwich Bread

Yes, you can make bread that is reminiscent of wheat yeast bread. A combination of flours and starches will give you the best results. It's best when toasted or grilled in a sandwich. Because there is no gluten in this dough, it doesn't rise long before you bake it; that helps keep the air in the loaf.

INGREDIENTS | MAKES 1 LOAF

1½ teaspoons active dry yeast

¼ cup warm water

¼ cup almond milk

1 tablespoon maple syrup

½ cup coconut flour

¾ cup almond flour

2 tablespoons hazelnut flour

2 tablespoons arrowroot powder

1 tablespoon ground flaxseed

½ teaspoon salt

2½ tablespoons Ener-G Egg Replacer mixed with ⅔ cup water

¼ cup puréed canned pears

1 tablespoon olive oil

1. Preheat oven to 350°F. Line a baking sheet with parchment paper and set aside.

2. In small bowl, combine yeast, warm water, almond milk, and maple syrup and mix. Let stand for 5 minutes until foamy.

3. In a large bowl, combine coconut flour, almond flour, hazelnut flour, arrowroot powder, ground flaxseed, and salt and mix until well combined.

4. Add yeast mixture, egg replacer mixture, pears, and olive oil. Mix well. Form into a long loaf shape on the prepared baking sheet. Let stand for 10 minutes.

5. Bake for 30–40 minutes or until the bread sounds hollow when tapped with fingers. You can briefly broil this bread for a golden brown color. Let cool on wire rack. Store in airtight container at room temperature.

Carrot and Date Salad

If you're used to carrot and raisin salads made with pineapple and drowning in mayonnaise, this lighter version with tahini, dates, and mandarin oranges will be a welcome change.

INGREDIENTS | SERVES 4

⅓ cup tahini

1 tablespoon olive oil

2 tablespoons maple syrup

3 tablespoons lemon juice

¼ teaspoon salt

4 large carrots, peeled and grated

½ cup chopped dates

3 medium mandarin oranges or clementines, peeled and sectioned

⅓ cup unsweetened coconut flakes

1. In a small bowl, whisk together tahini, olive oil, maple syrup, lemon juice, and salt.

2. Place carrots in a large bowl, and toss well with tahini mixture. Add dates, oranges, and coconut flakes and combine well.

3. Allow to sit for at least 1 hour before serving to soften carrots and dates. Toss again before serving.

Avocado-Watermelon Salad

This salad is packed with flavor. The watermelon adds a sweet touch to an otherwise plain salad.

INGREDIENTS | SERVES 4

2 large avocados, pitted, peeled, and diced

4 cups cubed watermelon

4 cups fresh baby spinach leaves

½ cup walnut oil

Juice of 1 medium lime

½ teaspoon sweet paprika

In a medium bowl, combine all ingredients. Mix well and serve.

Mushroom and Bean Salad

Mushrooms are delicious and so good for you. They are high in vitamin D—which is surprising since they're grown in the dark—and a good source of the B vitamin complex. More unusual types include fan-shaped chanterelles, brown and meaty cremini, earthy morels, rich portobello, tender oyster, beautiful hen of the woods, and delicate enoki. Choose a variety for this delicious salad.

INGREDIENTS | SERVES 4–6

¼ cup olive oil

3 tablespoons lemon juice

2 tablespoons Dijon mustard

1 tablespoon horseradish

½ teaspoon salt

⅛ teaspoon ground black pepper

1 tablespoon chopped fresh dill

1 cup sliced cremini mushrooms

1 cup sliced chanterelle mushrooms

1 cup sliced button mushrooms

1 cup sliced oyster mushrooms

2 cups trimmed green beans

2 cups trimmed wax beans

6 cups mixed salad greens

1. In large salad bowl, combine olive oil, lemon juice, mustard, horseradish, salt, pepper, and dill and whisk until combined. Add mushrooms and toss to coat.

2. Steam green beans and wax beans over simmering water until tender, about 7–8 minutes. Drain well.

3. Add beans to mushroom mixture and toss to coat. Serve on mixed salad greens.

Loaded Broccoli Salad

This salad really is a meal-in-one. The vegetables, nuts, and seeds provide your body with the complete protein you need. And it's delicious, flavorful, and full of color and texture. If you'd like, add some sliced fresh fruit to serve on the side.

INGREDIENTS | SERVES 4

1 head broccoli

1 pound green beans, trimmed and cut in half

1 (8-ounce) package mushrooms, sliced

1 medium red bell pepper, seeded and chopped

1 cup chopped walnuts

½ cup sunflower seeds

¼ cup sliced green onions

½ cup sliced black olives

⅓ cup olive oil

¼ cup lemon juice

3 tablespoons grainy mustard

½ teaspoon salt

⅛ teaspoon ground black pepper

½ cup chopped fresh parsley

2 tablespoons chopped fresh dill

1. Remove florets from broccoli. Peel broccoli stems and slice into ½" rounds.

2. Bring a large pot of water to a boil. Add broccoli stems; cook for 2 minutes. Add florets and cook for 2–3 minutes more or until tender. Remove with a large strainer and plunge into ice water.

3. Cook beans in boiling water until crisp-tender, about 4–5 minutes. Remove and plunge into ice water.

4. Drain cooked vegetables well and place in large serving bowl. Add mushrooms, bell pepper, walnuts, sunflower seeds, green onions, and olives and toss.

5. In small bowl, combine olive oil, lemon juice, mustard, salt, and pepper and mix. Pour over salad and toss to coat. Top with parsley and dill and serve.

Beet and Cauliflower Salad

This beautiful salad has such gorgeous colors, it's like a painting! And it's very good for you. Beets are a great source of antioxidants that help reduce the risk of cancer. They are also a great source of folate, magnesium, and potassium. Just remember to wear gloves when you work with beets, or your hands will be stained red for days!

INGREDIENTS | SERVES 4

4 large beets

½ cup water

¼ cup extra-virgin olive oil

1 shallot, minced

2 tablespoons apple cider vinegar

2 tablespoons coconut milk

1 tablespoon maple syrup

½ teaspoon salt

⅛ teaspoon ground black pepper

6 cups mixed salad greens

1 head cauliflower, broken into florets

½ cup toasted pumpkin or sunflower seeds

½ cup sliced fresh basil leaves

1. Preheat oven to 375°F. Place beets in a baking dish. Add water, cover tightly, and bake for about 65–75 minutes or until a knife slides easily into a beet. Remove from baking dish and let cool on wire rack.

2. When beets are cool, peel them and cut into ½" cubes. Set aside.

3. In salad bowl, combine olive oil, shallot, vinegar, coconut milk, maple syrup, salt, and pepper and mix well. Add greens and toss to coat.

4. Add beets and toss to coat.

5. Top with cauliflower florets, seeds, and basil and serve immediately.

Fruit and Nut Salad

Fruits and nuts make a delightful salad with excellent flavor and texture. You can use any fruits that look good in the market, and any nuts you like. Put this salad together right before serving; it doesn't keep well in the fridge.

INGREDIENTS | SERVES 4

1 tablespoon hazelnut oil

2 tablespoons olive oil

2 tablespoons lemon juice

2 tablespoons chopped fresh basil leaves

1 tablespoon chopped fresh mint leaves

¼ teaspoon salt

2 cups sliced strawberries

2 cups blueberries

2 cups cubed watermelon

½ cup chopped toasted hazelnuts

¼ cup toasted pine nuts

1. In large bowl, combine both oils, lemon juice, basil, mint, and salt and whisk until combined.

2. Add fruits and toss gently until coated. Top with nuts and serve immediately.

Cauliflower "Rice" Salad

Cauliflower "rice" makes a delightful base for a salad. The shreds are very briefly cooked to give them more of a cooked rice texture, but you can leave them raw if you'd like.

INGREDIENTS | SERVES 4

1 head cauliflower, shredded

4 tablespoons lemon juice, divided

1 tablespoon coconut oil

4 stalks celery, sliced

1 medium yellow bell pepper, seeded and chopped

2 medium carrots, peeled and shredded

⅓ cup finely chopped dill pickle

⅓ cup extra-virgin olive oil

1 tablespoon maple syrup

1 tablespoon chopped fresh dill

¼ teaspoon salt

⅛ teaspoon ground black pepper

1. Toss shredded cauliflower with 1 tablespoon lemon juice.

2. Heat coconut oil in skillet over medium heat. Add shredded cauliflower and cook for 1–2 minutes or until crisp-tender. Scrape cauliflower into a bowl and set aside to cool for 15 minutes.

3. Stir celery, bell pepper, carrots, and dill pickle into cauliflower.

4. In small bowl, combine olive oil, remaining 3 tablespoons lemon juice, maple syrup, dill, salt, and pepper and mix well. Pour over salad and stir to coat. Cover and chill for 1–3 hours before serving.

Mediterranean Salad

Olives, lemon, artichokes, red onion, and cucumbers combine in this easy and fresh-tasting salad. Serve with your favorite beverage and dream of the Mediterranean Sea!

INGREDIENTS | SERVES 4

¼ cup extra-virgin olive oil

2 tablespoons lemon juice

1 tablespoon Dijon mustard

1 clove garlic, peeled and minced

½ teaspoon dried oregano

¼ teaspoon salt

⅛ teaspoon ground black pepper

2 cups chopped curly endive

2 cups chopped butter lettuce

1 cup baby spinach leaves

1 (14-ounce) can plain artichokes, drained and sliced

1 small red onion, peeled and chopped

1 large cucumber, peeled, seeded, and chopped

½ cup pitted black olives

1. In large salad bowl, combine olive oil, lemon juice, mustard, garlic, oregano, salt, and pepper and mix well.

2. Add endive, lettuce, and spinach and toss to coat.

3. Top with artichokes, red onion, cucumber, and black olives, toss to coat, and serve.

Stuffed Tomatoes

These tomatoes are packed with flavor. They're perfect for a summertime lunch.

INGREDIENTS | SERVES 3

3 large beefsteak tomatoes
6 small button mushrooms, sliced
4 cloves garlic, peeled and minced
6 sun-dried tomatoes, chopped
1 teaspoon ground black pepper
½ teaspoon paprika
1 teaspoon thyme
8 leaves fresh basil, torn

1. Preheat oven to 350°F.

2. Hollow out tomatoes, reserving tomato pulp. Place tomatoes in a small baking dish.

3. In a medium bowl, mix tomato pulp with mushrooms, garlic, sun-dried tomatoes, pepper, paprika, thyme, and basil.

4. Fill tomatoes with stuffing mixture and bake for 25 minutes.

Avocado-Orange Lettuce Wraps

These light and delicious wraps taste like summer on a plate.

INGREDIENTS | SERVES 4

4 large romaine lettuce leaves
1 large navel orange, peeled and cut into ¼"-thick slices
2 large avocados, pitted, peeled, and sliced
1 (5-ounce) package alfalfa sprouts
Juice of 1 medium lemon

1. Arrange lettuce leaves on 4 plates.

2. Divide orange slices evenly over lettuce leaves. Stack avocado slices and sprouts on top of orange slices. Sprinkle with lemon juice.

3. Fold lettuce leaves in half and serve.

Asparagus and Avocado Lettuce Wraps

These crunchy wraps are perfect as an appetizer or a light side dish.

INGREDIENTS | SERVES 4

24 asparagus spears
1 large ripe avocado, pitted and peeled
1 tablespoon lime juice
1 clove garlic, peeled and minced
2 cups chopped tomato
2 tablespoons peeled, chopped red onion
4 whole romaine lettuce leaves
⅓ cup chopped cilantro leaves

Health Benefits of Asparagus

Asparagus is an often undervalued vegetable in the kitchen. This delicious stalk weighs in at a healthy 60 percent RDA of folic acid. Additionally, it is high in vitamins A, B_6, and C, as well as potassium.

1. In a medium saucepan over high heat, bring 2" water to a boil. Place asparagus in a steamer basket, place steamer in saucepan, and cover. Steam asparagus until just tender, about 5 minutes. Remove asparagus and immediately rinse in cold water. Drain thoroughly.

2. In a small bowl, mash avocado. Stir in lime juice and garlic. In another small bowl, stir together tomato and onion.

3. Lay lettuce leaves flat on a platter and spread each with a quarter of the avocado mixture. Top with the tomato mixture and cilantro leaves.

4. Fold in both sides and the bottom of each lettuce leaf before serving.

Spicy Spinach Smoothie

The taste of spinach can be altered by including it in certain combinations with other strong vegetables and fruits. This savory smoothie incorporates cilantro and garlic for a unique taste.

INGREDIENTS | MAKES 3–4 CUPS

1 cup spinach

1 medium tomato

1 stalk celery, chopped

2 tablespoons cilantro

1 clove garlic, peeled

2 cups water, divided

Garlic

Garlic may be one of the healthiest vegetables you can add to your smoothies. Studies credit it with fighting bladder, skin, colon, and stomach cancer. Eating one to three cloves per day is recommended for optimum results. Including garlic in your smoothies is an easy way to meet that recommendation.

1. Place spinach, tomato, celery, cilantro, garlic, and 1 cup water in a blender and blend until thoroughly combined.

2. Add remaining 1 cup water while blending until desired texture is achieved.

Sweet and Savory Beet Smoothie

Beets and their greens are filled with antioxidants and vitamins. Paired with flavorful carrots and cucumbers, they create a sweet and healthy smoothie you're sure to enjoy!

INGREDIENTS | MAKES 3–4 CUPS

1 cup chopped beet greens

2 medium beets, peeled and chopped

2 medium carrots, peeled and chopped

1 medium cucumber, peeled and chopped

2 cups water, divided

1. Place beet greens, beets, carrots, cucumber, and 1 cup water in a blender and blend until thoroughly combined.

2. Add remaining 1 cup water while blending until desired texture is achieved.

Beet Colors

Beets come in many colors, from deep red to orange. They also can be white. The Chioggia beet is called a candy cane beet because it has red and white rings. Small or medium beets are tenderer than larger ones. Roasted beets can be enjoyed on their own or flavored with some butter, salt, and pepper for a simple side dish.

The Green Bloody Mary

This green version of the Bloody Mary has all of the necessary ingredients to repair exactly what the alcoholic version destroys!

INGREDIENTS | MAKES 3–4 CUPS

1 cup chopped watercress
2 large tomatoes
2 stalks celery
½ large lemon, peeled
1 tablespoon horseradish
½ teaspoon cayenne pepper
1 cup water, divided

1. Place watercress, tomatoes, celery, lemon, horseradish, cayenne, and ½ cup water in a blender and blend until thoroughly combined.

2. Add remaining ½ cup water while blending until desired texture is achieved.

CHAPTER 4

Appetizers

Green and Black Olive Tapenade

Mediterranean olive tapenade can be used as a spread or dip for crisp vegetables. If you don't have a food processor, you can mash the ingredients together with a mortar and pestle or a large fork.

INGREDIENTS | MAKES 1 CUP

½ cup pitted green olives

¾ cup pitted black olives

2 cloves garlic, peeled

1 tablespoon capers

2 tablespoons lemon juice

2 tablespoons olive oil

¼ teaspoon oregano

¼ teaspoon ground black pepper

Process all ingredients in a food processor until almost smooth.

Eggplant Baba Ghanoush

Roasted eggplant makes a velvety dip full of Mediterranean flavors.

INGREDIENTS | MAKES 1½ CUPS

2 medium eggplants

3 tablespoons olive oil, divided

2 tablespoons lemon juice

¼ cup tahini

3 cloves garlic, peeled

½ teaspoon cumin

½ teaspoon chili powder

¼ teaspoon salt

1 tablespoon chopped fresh parsley

1. Preheat oven to 400°F. Slice eggplants in half lengthwise and prick skin several times with a fork. Place on a baking sheet and drizzle with 1 tablespoon olive oil. Bake for 30 minutes, or until soft. Allow to cool slightly.

2. Remove inner flesh and place in a bowl. Using a large fork or potato masher, mash eggplant together with remaining ingredients until almost smooth.

3. Serve at room temperature.

Homemade Tahini

If you're serving this as a Middle Eastern dip or spread, use the paprika for extra flavor, but leave it out if your tahini will be the basis for a salad dressing or another recipe. Tahini will keep for up to one month in the refrigerator in a tightly sealed container, or store it in the freezer and thaw before using.

INGREDIENTS | MAKES 1 CUP

2 cups sesame seeds
½ cup olive oil
½ teaspoon paprika

1. Heat oven to 350°F.

2. Spread sesame seeds in a thin layer on a baking sheet and toast for 5 minutes in the oven, shaking the sheet once to mix. Cool.

3. Process sesame seeds with oil in a food processor or blender until thick and creamy. You may need a little more or less than ½ cup oil. Garnish with paprika.

Roasted Parsnip Chips

Parsnips have a subtly sweet taste and a lower glycemic load than potatoes. They make a perfect chip for dipping.

INGREDIENTS | SERVES 6

6 large parsnips, peeled and cut diagonally into thin slices
3 tablespoons olive oil
⅛ teaspoon nutmeg
1 teaspoon cinnamon

1. Preheat oven to 400°F. Spray a baking sheet with cooking spray.

2. In a large bowl, combine parsnips, olive oil, and spices and stir to coat.

3. Arrange parsnips on baking sheet in a single layer and cook for 30 minutes. Remove from oven and turn on broiler. Broil chips for 5 minutes. Serve warm or at room temperature.

Mango Citrus Salsa

Salsa has many uses, and this recipe adds color and variety to an old standby.

INGREDIENTS | MAKES 2 CUPS

1 large mango, peeled, pitted, and chopped

2 medium tangerines, peeled and chopped

½ medium red bell pepper, seeded and chopped

½ small red onion, peeled and minced

3 cloves garlic, peeled and minced

½ medium jalapeño pepper, seeded and minced

2 tablespoons lime juice

½ teaspoon salt

¼ teaspoon ground black pepper

3 tablespoons chopped fresh cilantro

Gently toss together all ingredients in a large bowl. Allow to sit for at least 15 minutes before serving to allow flavors to mingle.

Two-Tomato Salsa

This salsa is sure to be a winner at any party. Serve it with Roasted Parsnip Chips (see recipe in this chapter) for a great appetizer before dinner.

INGREDIENTS | SERVES 2

½ cup chopped fresh cilantro

1½ cups chopped tomatoes

¼ cup chopped sun-dried tomatoes

½ cup olive oil

2 teaspoons lime juice

1 teaspoon minced fresh ginger

1½ teaspoons minced garlic

1 teaspoon minced jalapeño pepper

Combine all ingredients in a food processor and pulse quickly to blend. Salsa should have a slightly chunky texture.

Melon Salsa

Salsa is always a favorite at parties. This sweet melon salsa is a new take on the more traditional favorites.

INGREDIENTS | SERVES 4

3 large tomatoes, seeded and finely diced

½ large honeydew melon, peeled, seeded, and diced

1 medium cantaloupe, peeled, seeded, and diced

1 cup peeled, diced red onion

1 small jalapeño pepper, seeded and minced

½ cup chopped fresh cilantro

Juice of 1 large lime

In a large serving bowl, combine all ingredients and mix well. Chill for 4 hours before serving.

Melons

Melons have a relatively low sugar content, compared to other fruits, and half of a cantaloupe is only one serving. That makes it a good choice when you're watching calories or trying to limit fruit servings per day.

Fresh Pepper Salsa

Tomatoes are a great source of the antioxidant vitamin C. You can also get creative and make your salsa with other vegetables, fruits, and spices.

INGREDIENTS | YIELDS 1 PINT

1 medium yellow bell pepper, seeded, and chopped

1 medium orange bell pepper, seeded, and chopped

2 small poblano chilies, seeded and chopped

2 small Anaheim chilies, seeded and chopped

2 medium jalapeño peppers, seeded and chopped

2 cloves garlic, peeled

¼ medium red onion, peeled

Juice of ½ medium lime

1 teaspoon ground black pepper

2 tablespoons olive oil

¼ cup chopped cilantro

1. Place peppers, garlic, onion, lime juice, and black pepper in a food processor and pulse until slightly chunky.

2. In a medium saucepan, heat oil over high heat until slightly smoking. Add pepper mixture and cook for 8–10 minutes, stirring occasionally.

3. Remove from heat and sprinkle with cilantro. Serve hot, cold, or at room temperature.

Classic Guacamole

Guacamole is a favorite party appetizer, but it also packs a major healthy punch.

INGREDIENTS | SERVES 4

2 large ripe avocados, pitted, peeled, and coarsely chopped

1 small white onion, peeled and diced

1 medium tomato, diced

1 medium jalapeño pepper, seeded and thinly sliced

Juice of 1 medium lime

Gently combine all ingredients in a serving bowl and serve as a salad or dip.

Avocados 101

Avocados are high in the good, anti-inflammatory, monounsaturated type of fat. They are also favorably high in fiber, potassium, many B vitamins, and vitamin E. Avocados darken easily when exposed to air, so it is best to save any leftovers with the pits and keep them in a tightly sealed container in the refrigerator. Lemon or lime juice in recipes will also keep discoloration at bay.

Exotic Fruit Guacamole

Papaya and mango add an exotic, sweet-and-sour twist to a traditional dish.

INGREDIENTS | SERVES 4

1 medium papaya, peeled, pitted, and cubed

1 medium mango, peeled, pitted, and cubed

1 medium ripe avocado, pitted, peeled, and diced

1 tablespoon lime juice

2 cups diced, seeded tomato

¼ cup peeled, diced red onion

2 tablespoons minced fresh cilantro

1 teaspoon finely chopped jalapeño pepper

1 clove garlic, peeled and minced

Combine all ingredients in a medium bowl. Mix well and serve.

Papaya, "Fruit of the Angels"

One papaya contains over 300 percent of your daily vitamin C requirement and almost 30 percent of the recommended daily intake of folate. It's a rich source of potassium and vitamins A, E, and K, too.

Vegetable Kebabs

Serve these kebabs as an appetizer at parties so your guests can easily handle the food without using cutlery.

INGREDIENTS | SERVES 6

Wooden skewers, cut in half and soaked in water for at least 1 hour

12 scallions, trimmed

1 large red pepper, seeded and cut into large chunks

1 large yellow pepper, seeded and cut into large chunks

1 large green pepper, seeded and cut into large chunks

12 large button mushrooms

1 tablespoon olive oil

Freshly ground black pepper

1. Preheat grill or broiler.

2. Thread vegetables onto skewers, and brush all sides of vegetables with oil. Season with pepper.

3. Place skewers on the grill or under the broiler, paying close attention as they cook, as they can easily burn. Cook about 10 minutes, until vegetables are fork tender.

Soaking the Skewers

When using wooden skewers, always soak them in water for an hour before spearing the food items. Soaking the skewers allows you to place them on the grill for a time without them burning.

CHAPTER 5

Salads and Dressings

Raspberry Vinaigrette

Create a colorful and inviting salad with this purplish dressing. Dress up a plain fruit salad, or toss some cranberries, pine nuts, and baby spinach with this vinaigrette for a gourmet touch.

INGREDIENTS | MAKES 1¼ CUPS

¼ cup apple cider vinegar
2 tablespoons lime juice
¼ cup raspberry purée
2 tablespoons Dijon mustard
1 tablespoon maple syrup
¾ cup olive oil
1 teaspoon salt
½ teaspoon ground black pepper

1. Process together vinegar, lime juice, raspberry purée, mustard, and maple syrup in a food processor or blender until smooth.

2. Slowly add olive oil a few drops at a time on high speed to allow oil to emulsify. Season with salt and pepper.

Basic Balsamic Vinaigrette

No need to purchase expensive and sugar-laden salad dressings at the grocery store! This simple vinaigrette will serve you well for a last-minute salad dressing.

INGREDIENTS | MAKES 1 CUP

¼ cup apple cider vinegar
¾ cup olive oil
1 tablespoon Dijon mustard
¼ teaspoon salt
⅛ teaspoon ground black pepper
½ teaspoon dried basil
½ teaspoon dried parsley

In a small bowl, whisk together all ingredients with a fork until well combined.

Tarragon Vinaigrette

Fresh tarragon is a wonderful herb that adds flavor to any dish. It's especially good in salad dressings. You can make a quantity of this recipe and store it in the fridge, covered, for up to two weeks. Just shake it before using it to dress spinach or lettuce salads.

INGREDIENTS | MAKES 1 CUP

2 tablespoons Dijon mustard
2 tablespoons apple cider vinegar
1 tablespoon lemon juice
4 teaspoons chopped fresh tarragon
⅔ cup olive oil
¼ teaspoon salt

In small jar with screw-on lid, combine all ingredients. Cover jar tightly and shake well. Store in refrigerator; shake before each use.

Sweet Cinnamon Salad Dressing

This delicious salad dressing is good on a plain spinach salad, or try it on a fruit salad made of blueberries, apples, cherries, grapes, and sliced figs. It keeps well in the fridge and is easy to whip up when you get a craving for a fresh fruit salad.

INGREDIENTS | MAKES ¾ CUP

⅓ cup maple syrup
¼ cup apple cider vinegar
2 tablespoons hazelnut oil
3 tablespoons olive oil
½ teaspoon cinnamon
Pinch cardamom
Pinch salt

In small jar with a tight-fitting lid, combine all ingredients and shake well. Use immediately, or cover and store in the refrigerator for up to 1 week.

French Dressing

Bottled commercial French dressing is loaded with all kinds of sweeteners like high fructose corn syrup as well as xanthan gum and food starch thickeners—not what you want on the Vegan Paleo diet. This easy recipe tastes much better than any French dressing you've had before!

INGREDIENTS | MAKES 1¼ CUPS

1 small onion, peeled and finely chopped

2 cloves garlic, peeled and minced

¼ cup apple cider vinegar

1 tablespoon lemon juice

2 tablespoons tomato paste

2 tablespoons Homemade Ketchup (see recipe in Chapter 12)

1 tablespoon Dijon mustard

2½ tablespoons maple syrup

½ cup olive oil

½ teaspoon smoked paprika

¼ teaspoon salt

⅛ teaspoon ground white pepper

1. Combine all ingredients in a food processor or blender. Cover and blend until smooth.

2. Cover and refrigerate for 2–3 hours to let flavors blend. Store tightly covered in the refrigerator for up to 5 days.

Curry Salad Dressing

This dressing goes well on any salad and has a nice flavor from the curry powder.

INGREDIENTS | SERVES 1

3 tablespoons olive oil

Juice of 1 medium lime

1 teaspoon curry powder

½ teaspoon ground black pepper

1 teaspoon dried basil

Combine all ingredients in a small bowl and stir well.

Asian Dressing

When you crave the taste of Chinese food, add this dressing to any plain dish to spice things up a bit.

INGREDIENTS | SERVES 4

2 tablespoons olive oil

2 tablespoons sesame oil

2 tablespoons tahini paste

½ teaspoon ground black pepper

1 teaspoon dried thyme leaves

Combine all ingredients in a small bowl and stir well.

Italian Dressing

Try doubling this recipe and storing the dressing in a glass jar. It will keep for several days and is much better than the supermarket varieties.

INGREDIENTS | MAKES 1 CUP

⅓ cup apple cider vinegar

½ teaspoon dry mustard

1 teaspoon lemon juice

2 cloves garlic, peeled and chopped

1 teaspoon dried oregano or 1 tablespoon fresh oregano leaves

½ teaspoon salt

½ teaspoon ground black pepper

½ cup extra-virgin olive oil

Place all ingredients except oil in a blender. With the blender running on a medium setting, slowly pour in oil. Blend until very smooth. Serve immediately on salad or cover and store in the refrigerator for up to 7 days.

Spicy Sweet Cucumber Salad

This cucumber salad is cool and refreshing, but with a bit of spice. Enjoy it as a healthy afternoon snack or as a fresh accompaniment to take-out.

INGREDIENTS | SERVES 2

2 medium cucumbers, peeled and thinly sliced

¾ teaspoon salt

¼ cup apple cider vinegar

1 tablespoon maple syrup

1 teaspoon sesame oil

¼ teaspoon red pepper flakes

½ medium onion, peeled and thinly sliced

1. In a large shallow container or on a baking sheet, spread cucumbers in a single layer and sprinkle with salt. Allow to sit at least 10 minutes.

2. Drain excess water from cucumbers. Transfer cucumbers to a medium bowl.

3. In a small bowl, whisk together vinegar, maple syrup, oil, and red pepper flakes.

4. Pour dressing over cucumbers, add onion, and toss gently.

5. Allow to sit at least 10 minutes before serving to allow flavors to mingle.

Tangerine and Mint Salad

Fennel and mint is a wonderful combination, but the sweet tangerines will carry the salad if you can't find fennel. A small drizzle of gourmet oil, if you have some, would kick up the flavor even more. Try walnut or avocado oil.

INGREDIENTS | SERVES 2

1 medium head green leaf lettuce, chopped

2 tablespoons chopped fresh mint

2 large tangerines, clementines, or satsuma oranges, peeled and sectioned

⅓ cup chopped walnuts

1 bulb fennel, thinly sliced

2 tablespoons olive oil

1 teaspoon salt

½ teaspoon ground black pepper

Gently toss together lettuce, mint, tangerines, walnuts, and sliced fennel. Drizzle with olive oil, season with salt and pepper, and serve immediately.

Homemade Flavored Oils

A flavored oil will beautify your kitchen and add flavor to your food. Simply combine several of your favorite herbs, whole garlic cloves, peppercorns, dried lemon or orange zest, and/or dried chilies with a quality olive oil. For safety's sake, avoid fresh herbs and zests. Always use dried. Oils infused with dried herbs will keep for up to one year, while fresh herbs can cause spoilage after less than a week.

Sweet Red Salad with Strawberries and Beets

*Colorful and nutritious, this vibrant red salad can be made with roasted
or canned beets or even raw grated beets if you prefer.*

INGREDIENTS | SERVES 4

3–4 small beets, peeled and chopped
5 cups baby spinach
1 cup sliced strawberries
½ cup chopped pecans
¼ cup olive oil
2 tablespoons apple cider vinegar
2 tablespoons maple syrup
2 tablespoons orange juice
1 teaspoon salt
½ teaspoon ground black pepper

1. Place beets in a medium saucepan and cover with water. Boil beets in water until soft, about 20 minutes. Drain beets and allow to cool completely.

2. In a large bowl, combine spinach, strawberries, pecans, and cooled beets.

3. In a separate small bowl, whisk together olive oil, vinegar, maple syrup, and orange juice and pour over salad, tossing well to coat.

4. Season with salt and pepper.

Ribbon Salad

Your vegetable peeler can turn ordinary root vegetables and squash into a gorgeous side salad. This recipe takes a bit of time, but the end result is just beautiful and very delicious. You can also use a spiralizer to make noodle shapes.

INGREDIENTS | SERVES 6

2 medium zucchini
2 large carrots, peeled
2 medium yellow summer squash
2 tablespoons olive oil
3 tablespoons lemon juice
1 tablespoon Dijon mustard
1 tablespoon chopped fresh dill
½ teaspoon salt
⅛ teaspoon ground black pepper

1. Rinse vegetables and pat dry; cut off ends. Using a vegetable peeler or a mandoline, shave vegetables into thin, wide ribbons. Don't shave the seedy cores of the zucchini and squash; discard those when you get to them.

2. In a large bowl, combine olive oil, lemon juice, mustard, dill, salt, and pepper and mix well. Add vegetable ribbons and toss to coat. Serve immediately, or cover and refrigerate for up to 24 hours before serving.

Broccoli, Pine Nut, and Apple Salad

This quick little salad will tide you over until your next meal. The broccoli and apple taste great together, and the toasted pine nuts add a little bit of crunch.

INGREDIENTS | SERVES 2

4 tablespoons olive oil
¾ cup pine nuts
2 cups broccoli florets
2 cups cored, diced Granny Smith apples
Juice of 1 large lemon

1. Heat olive oil in a small skillet over medium heat and sauté pine nuts until golden brown.

2. Mix broccoli and apples in a medium bowl. Add pine nuts and toss.

3. Squeeze lemon juice over salad and serve.

Red Pepper and Fennel Salad

Fennel has a fantastic licorice flavor that blends nicely with nuts. The red pepper adds a flash of color and a bit of sweetness to the mix.

INGREDIENTS | SERVES 1

2 tablespoons olive oil
⅓ cup pine nuts
3 tablespoons sesame seeds
1 medium red bell pepper, seeded and halved
6 leaves romaine lettuce, shredded
½ medium bulb fennel, trimmed and diced
1 tablespoon walnut oil
Juice from 1 medium lime
½ teaspoon ground black pepper

Walnut Oil

Walnut oil cannot withstand high heat, so it's best to add it to food that has been cooked or is served raw, such as a salad. If you choose to cook with it, use a lower flame to avoid burning the oil.

1. Preheat broiler.

2. In a medium skillet, heat olive oil over medium heat. Sauté pine nuts and sesame seeds for 5 minutes.

3. Grill pepper under the broiler until the skin is blackened and the flesh has softened slightly. Place pepper halves in a paper bag to cool slightly. When cool enough to handle, remove skin and slice into strips.

4. Combine red pepper slices, lettuce, and fennel in a large salad bowl.

5. Add walnut oil, lime juice, and black pepper. Mix well to combine. Top with pine nut mixture before serving.

Root Vegetable Salad

This root salad has a nice texture and color. It will go well with any traditional fall or winter dish and will make your home smell like you're cooking a holiday meal.

INGREDIENTS | SERVES 4

1 large rutabaga, peeled and cubed
1 large turnip, peeled and cubed
6 medium parsnips, peeled and cubed
3 tablespoons olive oil
1 tablespoon cinnamon
3 cloves garlic, peeled and chopped
1 tablespoon ground ginger
1 teaspoon ground black pepper

1. Preheat oven to 400°F.

2. Place rutabaga, turnip, and parsnips in a large roasting pan and drizzle with olive oil. Sprinkle with cinnamon, garlic, ginger, and pepper. Toss to coat.

3. Roast for 40–50 minutes or until toothpick slides through vegetables easily.

Mediterranean Tomato Salad

Use juicy tomatoes for this recipe, such as heirloom or beefsteak varieties. You can substitute orange bell pepper for the yellow if needed.

INGREDIENTS | SERVES 4

2 cups sliced tomatoes
1 cup chopped cucumber
⅓ cup seeded, diced yellow bell pepper
¼ cup sliced radishes
¼ cup chopped flat-leaf parsley
1 clove garlic, peeled and finely minced
1 tablespoon lemon juice
3 tablespoons extra-virgin olive oil
1 teaspoon salt
½ teaspoon ground black pepper
2 cups torn baby spinach leaves

1. In a large salad bowl, toss tomatoes, cucumber, bell pepper, radishes, and parsley together.

2. Sprinkle garlic, lemon juice, oil, salt, and pepper over salad. Toss to coat. Split spinach among four plates and top with tomato mixture. Serve immediately.

Kale and Sea Vegetables with Orange Sesame Dressing

This salad is a great appetizer for an Asian-themed meal.

INGREDIENTS | SERVES 4

¼ cup wakame seaweed

½ cup sea lettuce

3 cups chopped kale

½ teaspoon lemon juice

¼ cup orange juice

7 tablespoons sesame seeds, divided

1 tablespoon kelp powder

Sea Vegetables

Sea vegetables are among the most nutritious and mineral-rich foods on earth. Ocean water contains all the mineral elements known to man. For example, both kelp and dulse are excellent sources of iodine, which is an essential nutrient missing in most diets. Sea vegetables are dried and should be soaked in water to reconstitute before eating.

1. Soak wakame and sea lettuce in water for 30 minutes. Rinse vegetables and discard the soak water.

2. Place kale in a large bowl and sprinkle with lemon juice. Massage juice into kale until kale is wilted. Add wakame and sea lettuce.

3. Place orange juice, 6 tablespoons sesame seeds, and kelp powder in a blender and blend until smooth. Pour dressing over kelp mixture and toss to coat. Top with remaining sesame seeds.

Spring Greens with Berries

The acid in the lime juice breaks down the fat in the olive oil to make a flavorful dressing.

INGREDIENTS | SERVES 2

4 tablespoons lime juice

4 tablespoons olive oil

¼ teaspoon ground cumin

2 teaspoons minced jalapeño pepper

4 cups mixed baby greens

2 cups blackberries or raspberries

¼ cup peeled, thinly sliced red onion

1. Place lime juice, olive oil, cumin, and jalapeño in a blender and blend together until smooth.

2. In a large bowl, toss dressing with greens, berries, and onions and serve immediately.

Avocado Salad

This salad is the perfect choice on a hot summer day when you want something cold and satisfying.

INGREDIENTS | SERVES 4

2 medium avocados, peeled, pitted, and diced

1 small sweet onion, peeled and chopped

1 medium red bell pepper, seeded and chopped

1 large ripe tomato, chopped

¼ cup chopped fresh cilantro

Juice of ½ medium lime

Combine all ingredients in a medium bowl. Mix well and chill for at least 2 hours before serving.

Red Versus Green Peppers

Although green and red peppers are both healthy choices, red peppers contain a very high amount of vitamins A and C. One medium red pepper can contribute a whopping 75 percent of your daily value of vitamin A and 253 percent of vitamin C, compared with 9 percent vitamin A and 159 percent vitamin C per medium green pepper.

Crisp Avocado Salad

This recipe works well as a side dish for spicy Southwest or Mexican entrées.

INGREDIENTS | SERVES 4

3 cups shredded iceberg lettuce

2 cups pitted, peeled, chopped avocado

½ cup peeled, sliced red onion

1 (3-ounce) can sliced black olives

1 tablespoon lime juice

2 tablespoons toasted pine nuts

Toss lettuce, avocado, onion, and olives together in a large salad bowl. Sprinkle salad with lime juice. Toss well to coat. Top with pine nuts and serve.

Orange-Colored Salad

This healthful salad is beautiful as well as delicious.

INGREDIENTS | SERVES 4

3 cups cubed butternut squash

2 tablespoons olive oil, divided

2 medium carrots, peeled and shredded

2 cups diced papaya

2 tablespoons shredded fresh ginger

Juice of 1 medium lime

1 tablespoon maple syrup

1 teaspoon salt

½ teaspoon ground black pepper

1. Preheat oven to 425°F. Place squash on a large baking sheet and drizzle with 1 tablespoon olive oil. Roast for 15 minutes or until tender. Remove from oven and cool.

2. In a large salad bowl, combine squash, carrots, and papaya. Set aside.

3. In a small bowl, stir together ginger, lime juice, maple syrup, 1 tablespoon olive oil, salt, and pepper until well combined. Toss the dressing with the squash mixture and serve.

Crunchy Fruit Salad

Try this colorful salad after a workout. It will replenish glycogen and satisfy a sugar craving at the same time.

INGREDIENTS | SERVES 2

½ medium pineapple, peeled, cored, and cubed

1 medium papaya, cubed

1 medium banana, peeled and sliced

½ cup halved seedless grapes

1 tablespoon maple syrup

¼ cup chopped cashews

¼ cup unsweetened coconut flakes

Combine all ingredients in a large bowl, toss, and serve.

Seasonal Fruits

It is always best to eat foods that are native to your area and in season. If you buy fruits that are imported, be aware that they have traveled long distances and their freshness cannot be guaranteed.

Minty Blueberry Melon Salad

Seedless watermelons can sometimes have small white seeds scattered among the flesh. Use a fork to remove any noticeable seeds from the cubed watermelon before making the salad.

INGREDIENTS | SERVES 4

1½ cups cubed cantaloupe
1 cup cubed seedless watermelon
1 cup halved green grapes
¾ cup blueberries
1 tablespoon minced mint leaves
1 teaspoon minced flat-leaf parsley

1. In a large salad bowl, gently toss cantaloupe, watermelon, grapes, and blueberries together.

2. Add mint and parsley to salad. Toss to combine. Serve immediately or chill for up to 2 hours before serving.

Fire-Kissed Cantaloupe Salad

Garnish this light and spicy salad with fresh cilantro or a slice of mango. Serve it as a side or as a unique dessert.

INGREDIENTS | SERVES 4

2 tablespoons mango juice
1 tablespoon walnut oil
⅛ teaspoon chili powder
⅛ teaspoon sweet Hungarian paprika
⅛ teaspoon ground red pepper
3 cups cubed cantaloupe
½ cup peeled, diced red onion

1. Whisk mango juice, oil, chili powder, paprika, and red pepper together in a small bowl until oil is emulsified.

2. Place cantaloupe and red onion in a large bowl. Pour dressing over salad and toss well to coat. Cover salad and chill in refrigerator for 15 minutes. Remove bowl from refrigerator, toss salad gently again, and serve.

Sweet and Fruity Salad

This sweet, crunchy salad is perfect for a quick lunch.

INGREDIENTS | SERVES 1

2 cups shredded romaine lettuce

4 cherry tomatoes

½ cup cored, sliced Gala apple

2 tablespoons golden raisins

2 tablespoons diced mandarin oranges, peeled and diced

Combine all ingredients in a medium bowl and toss to combine.

Sweet Melon Salad

Melons are a great source of vitamin C, fiber, and water. This salad combines three different types of melons with a fresh mint dressing. It's luscious.

INGREDIENTS | SERVES 6

2 tablespoons lemon juice

2 tablespoons maple syrup

2 tablespoons coconut milk

2 tablespoons chopped fresh mint

Pinch salt

3 cups cubed cantaloupe

3 cups cubed watermelon

2 cups cubed honeydew melon

1. In large serving bowl, combine lemon juice, maple syrup, coconut milk, mint, and salt and mix well.

2. Add melons and stir gently to coat. Serve immediately, or cover and chill for up to 6 hours before serving.

Rainbow Fruit Salad

You can't go wrong with this salad—it's juicy, fresh, naturally low in fat and sodium, and cholesterol free. Enjoy it as a salad or as a dessert.

INGREDIENTS | SERVES 12

1 large mango, peeled and diced
2 cups fresh blueberries
1 cup sliced bananas
2 cups halved strawberries
2 cups halved seedless grapes
1 cup peeled, sliced nectarines
½ cup peeled, sliced kiwi fruit
⅓ cup orange juice
2 tablespoons lemon juice
1½ tablespoons maple syrup
¼ teaspoon ground ginger
⅛ teaspoon ground nutmeg

1. In a large bowl, gently toss mango, blueberries, bananas, strawberries, grapes, nectarines, and kiwi together.

2. In a small bowl, stir together orange juice, lemon juice, maple syrup, ginger, and nutmeg; mix well.

3. Chill fruit until needed, for up to 3 hours. Just before serving, pour orange sauce over fruit and toss gently to coat.

Arugula and Fennel Salad with Pomegranate

Pomegranates pack a high dose of beneficial, health-promoting antioxidants. They are in peak season October through January. If you can't find pomegranates, you can use dried cranberries.

INGREDIENTS | SERVES 4

2 large navel oranges, peeled and sliced into small pieces

1 large pomegranate, seeds and surrounding flesh only

4 cups arugula

1 cup thinly sliced fennel

4 tablespoons olive oil

½ teaspoon ground black pepper

1. Add orange pieces and pomegranate seeds to a large bowl.

2. Add arugula, fennel slices, olive oil, and pepper. Toss to coat and serve immediately.

Fennel Facts

Fennel, a crunchy and slightly sweet vegetable, is a popular Mediterranean ingredient. Fennel has a white or greenish-white bulb and long stalks with feathery green leaves stemming from the top. Fennel is closely related to cilantro, dill, carrots, and parsley.

Pineapple Onion Salad

This sweet and tangy salad does not keep well, so make sure to throw it together right before eating. If you prefer a little more zing, add another tablespoon of lime juice and a sprinkle of ground cayenne pepper.

INGREDIENTS | SERVES 4

1 cup pineapple chunks
½ cup peeled, chopped red onion
3 cups mixed baby greens
1 tablespoon lime juice

Place pineapple chunks, onion, and greens in a large salad bowl. Sprinkle with lime juice. Toss to coat and serve immediately.

Shaved Fennel Salad with Orange Sections and Toasted Hazelnuts

Tangelos, clementines, or any easily sectioned citrus will work wonderfully with this recipe.

INGREDIENTS | SERVES 6

6 large oranges, peeled
3 medium bulbs fennel, finely sliced
1 teaspoon finely chopped hazelnuts
⅓ cup orange juice
2 tablespoons extra-virgin olive oil
1 tablespoon orange zest

1. With a small paring knife, remove each section of the oranges and slice away membrane.

2. Form a mound of sliced fennel on each serving plate and arrange oranges on top. Sprinkle with nuts, then drizzle with orange juice and oil. Finish with a sprinkle of zest.

German Coleslaw

*Red or yellow peppers can be substituted here for the green peppers
to give this coleslaw a bit more color, like confetti!*

INGREDIENTS | SERVES 4

1 teaspoon celery seed

1½ cups lime juice

1½ teaspoons mustard seed

1 teaspoon turmeric

1 teaspoon lemon juice

8 cups shredded cabbage

2 medium green bell peppers, seeded
and finely chopped

1 large onion, peeled and
finely chopped

1. In a saucepan over high heat, bring celery seed, lime juice, mustard seed, turmeric, and lemon juice to a boil.

2. Place cabbage, bell peppers, and onion in a 2-quart or smaller baking dish with a cover.

3. Pour boiling liquid over vegetables. Cover and let stand for 2 hours. Serve at room temperature or chilled. This salad will keep crisp for 3–4 weeks in the refrigerator.

Apple Coleslaw

This coleslaw recipe is a refreshing and sweet alternative to the traditional coleslaw with mayonnaise. The sesame seeds give it a nice, nutty flavor.

INGREDIENTS | SERVES 4

2 cups packaged coleslaw mix

1 large unpeeled tart apple, cored and chopped

½ cup chopped celery

½ cup chopped green pepper

¼ cup flaxseed oil

2 tablespoons lemon juice

1 teaspoon sesame seeds

1. In a medium bowl combine coleslaw mix, apple, celery, and green pepper.

2. In a small bowl, whisk together remaining ingredients. Pour over coleslaw and toss to coat.

Seeds Versus Nuts

Nuts have a higher ratio of omega-6 to omega-3 fatty acids. Seeds, on the other hand, have a much different profile. Seeds have a much lower saturated fat content and are more easily digested by individuals with intestinal issues.

CHAPTER 6

Soups and Stocks

Basic Vegetable Stock

This versatile broth is low in sodium and high in disease-fighting phytonutrients. Try adding mushrooms for additional flavor.

INGREDIENTS | MAKES 1 GALLON

2 pounds yellow onions, peeled and roughly chopped

1 pound carrots, peeled and roughly chopped

1 pound celery, roughly chopped

1½ gallons water

1 bunch parsley stems, chopped

4 sprigs fresh thyme

2 bay leaves

10–20 peppercorns

1. Place onions, carrots, celery, and water in a large stockpot over medium heat; bring to a simmer and cook, uncovered, for 1½ hours.

2. Add parsley stems, thyme, bay leaves, and peppercorns, and continue to simmer, uncovered, for 45 minutes.

3. Remove from heat and strain stock. Discard solids. Stock can be refrigerated for 2–4 days or frozen for up to 3 months.

Homemade Stocks

Your homemade stocks give a special quality to all the dishes you use them in. Not only will the flavor of homemade stocks be better than that from purchased bases, but you will have added your own personal touch to the meal. Always cook them uncovered, as covering will cause them to become cloudy.

Roasted Vegetable Stock

Use this stock as a flavorful base for soups and stews or in other recipes as a flavorful alternative to water.

INGREDIENTS | MAKES 5 QUARTS

3 medium carrots, peeled and coarsely chopped

3 medium parsnips, peeled and coarsely chopped

3 large onions, peeled and quartered

3 whole turnips

3 rutabagas, quartered

3 medium bell peppers, seeded and halved

2 medium shallots, peeled

1 head garlic

1 bunch fresh thyme

1 bunch parsley

5 quarts water

1. Preheat oven to 425°F. Line a 9" × 13" baking pan with parchment paper. Arrange all the vegetables and herbs in the pan and roast for 30 minutes or until browned.

2. Add vegetables to a 6-quart slow cooker. Add 5 quarts of water and cover. Cook on low for 8–10 hours. Strain stock, discarding the solids. Freeze or refrigerate stock and use within 1–2 weeks.

Mushroom Stock

Shiitake mushrooms add a rich, bold flavor, and also provide a variety of beneficial phytonutrients. Be careful to not overcook this stock.

INGREDIENTS | MAKES 2 QUARTS

1 quart water

12 ounces white mushrooms

6 parsley stems (with leaves)

1 large onion, peeled and sliced

1 large leek (white part only)

1 stalk celery, sliced

2 ounces dried shiitake mushrooms

1 tablespoon minced garlic

1½ teaspoons black peppercorns

¾ teaspoon dried sage

¾ teaspoon dried thyme leaves

½ teaspoon ground black pepper

1. Combine all ingredients except ground pepper in a 6-quart slow cooker; cover and cook on low for 6–8 hours.

2. Strain, discarding solids; season with ground pepper. Serve immediately, refrigerate and use within 1–2 weeks, or freeze.

Shiitake and Garlic Broth

Shiitake mushrooms transform ordinary broth into a rich stock with a deep flavor.

INGREDIENTS | YIELDS 6 CUPS

⅓ cup dried shiitake mushrooms

6 cups water

2 cloves garlic, peeled and smashed

1 bay leaf

½ teaspoon thyme

½ medium onion, peeled and chopped

1. Combine all ingredients in a large soup pot or stockpot and bring to a slow simmer over medium heat.

2. Cover and allow to cook for 30–40 minutes.

3. Strain broth before using.

Vegetarian Dashi

To turn this into a Japanese dashi stock for miso and noodle soups, omit the bay leaf and thyme and add a generous amount of seaweed, preferably kombu, if you can find it!

Tomato Soup

Tomato soup is an old-fashioned comfort food. This recipe is not made with cream or butter, but it has a smooth, rich taste you'll love.

INGREDIENTS | SERVES 4

4 cups chopped tomatoes

½ cup peeled, chopped onion

4 whole cloves

2 cups Basic Vegetable Stock (see recipe in this chapter)

2 tablespoons olive oil

2 tablespoons almond flour

Juice from 1 medium lime

1. In a stockpot, combine tomatoes, onion, cloves, and vegetable stock over medium-high heat. Bring to a boil, reduce heat to medium-low, and simmer for about 20 minutes.

2. Remove from heat and strain into large bowl. Discard solids.

3. In the now-empty stockpot, combine olive oil and almond flour. Stir until mixture thickens.

4. Gradually whisk in tomato mixture and stir in lime juice.

Zucchini Soup

This smooth and soothing blend of fresh herbs and spices is perfect for a cold late-autumn day.

INGREDIENTS | SERVES 8

4 cups sliced zucchini

4 cups Basic Vegetable Stock (see recipe in this chapter)

4 cloves garlic, peeled and minced

2 tablespoons lime juice

2 teaspoons curry powder

1 teaspoon dried marjoram leaves

¼ teaspoon celery seeds

½ cup coconut milk

¼ teaspoon cayenne pepper

1 teaspoon paprika

1. Combine all ingredients except coconut milk, cayenne pepper, and paprika in a 4–6-quart slow cooker, and cook on high for 3–4 hours.

2. Process zucchini mixture with coconut milk in a blender until combined.

3. Season with cayenne pepper. Sprinkle with paprika and serve warm.

Scallion Chive Soup

Chive adds a sweet, mild oniony taste to this lovely green soup.

INGREDIENTS | SERVES 2

3 teaspoons olive oil
½ cup shredded zucchini
½ cup chopped shallots
1 clove garlic, peeled and minced
1 cup chopped scallions
½ cup chopped chives
2 cups Basic Vegetable Stock (see recipe in this chapter)
½ cup water

Chive As Insect Repellent

Chive has such a strong scent that it can be used in gardens as an insect repellent. Garlic has also been known to be an effective defense against pests.

1. Heat olive oil in a soup pot or Dutch oven over medium-low heat. Sauté zucchini, shallots, and garlic in oil for 3–5 minutes. Add scallions and chives and cook for 2 minutes more.

2. Add vegetable stock and water. Increase heat to high and bring to a boil. Reduce heat to low and simmer for 5 minutes.

3. In batches, purée soup in blender or food processor.

Carrot-Lemon Soup

This is a great anytime soup and can be served either hot or cold.

INGREDIENTS | SERVES 6

3 tablespoons olive oil

2 pounds carrots, peeled and diced

2 large yellow onions, peeled and diced

2 cloves garlic, peeled and minced

6 cups Basic Vegetable Stock (see recipe in this chapter) or low-sodium canned vegetable stock

1 teaspoon minced fresh ginger

Juice and zest from 1 large lemon

½ teaspoon ground black pepper

3 scallions, thinly sliced

1. Heat oil in a large stockpot over medium heat. Sauté carrots, onions, and garlic until softened, about 8 minutes.

2. Add stock and bring to a boil over high heat. Reduce heat to low and simmer for approximately 1 hour. Add ginger, lemon juice, and zest. Season with pepper.

3. Garnish with scallions. Serve hot or refrigerate for at least 4 hours.

Lemon Know-How

The average lemon contains approximately 3 tablespoons of juice. Allow lemons to come to room temperature before squeezing to maximize the amount of juice extracted.

Easy Roasted Tomato Soup

Use the freshest, ripest, juiciest red tomatoes you can find for this super-easy recipe. If you find that you need a bit more spice, add a spoonful of nutritional yeast, a dash of cayenne pepper, or an extra shake of salt and ground black pepper.

INGREDIENTS | SERVES 4

6 large tomatoes, cored and halved

1 small onion, peeled and quartered

4 cloves garlic, peeled

2 tablespoons olive oil

1¼ cups almond milk

2 tablespoons chopped fresh basil

1½ teaspoons apple cider vinegar

¾ teaspoon salt

¼ teaspoon ground black pepper

1. Preheat oven to 425°F.

2. Place tomatoes, onion, and garlic on baking sheet and drizzle with olive oil. Roast in the oven for 45 minutes–1 hour until very soft.

3. Carefully transfer tomatoes, onion, and garlic to a blender, including any juices on the baking sheet. Add remaining ingredients and purée until almost smooth.

4. Pour mixture into a large saucepan and heat over low heat for 2 minutes until hot.

Celery Mushroom Soup

Soups can be thick and hearty, or they can be delicate. This is the delicate type of soup. It's good for when you're feeling a bit under the weather, and it's great for packing into a thermos for lunch, either for school or for work. For best results, make your own vegetable stock for this recipe. Canned and boxed stocks just don't compare to homemade.

INGREDIENTS | SERVES 6

2 tablespoons olive oil

1 medium shallot, peeled and finely minced

1 (8-ounce) package cremini mushrooms, sliced

1 medium bunch celery, trimmed and thinly sliced

6 cups Basic Vegetable Stock or Roasted Vegetable Stock (see recipes in this chapter)

1 teaspoon dried thyme leaves

1 teaspoon salt

⅛ teaspoon ground white pepper

1 tablespoon lemon juice

1. In large pot, heat olive oil over medium heat. Add shallot; cook until softened, about 3 minutes.

2. Add mushrooms; cook and stir until mushrooms give up their liquid, about 8 minutes.

3. Add celery and cook for 4 minutes longer. Add stock, thyme, salt, and pepper, and bring to a simmer.

4. Cover pot, reduce heat to low, and simmer for 15–20 minutes or until soup is blended. Stir in lemon juice and serve immediately.

Southwest Almond Soup

This soup is spicy, thick, and rich, with a wonderful texture and flavor combination.

INGREDIENTS | SERVES 6

3 tablespoons olive oil

1 medium onion, peeled and chopped

2 cloves garlic, peeled and minced

1 medium jalapeño pepper, seeded and minced

3 tablespoons almond flour

1 teaspoon ground cumin

5 cups Basic Vegetable Stock (see recipe in this chapter)

⅔ cup almond butter

⅓ cup almond milk

½ teaspoon salt

⅛ teaspoon ground black pepper

⅔ cup sliced almonds, toasted

½ cup Kale Pesto (see recipe in Chapter 12)

1. In large soup pot, heat olive oil over medium heat. Add onion, garlic, and jalapeño; cook and stir for 5 minutes.

2. Add almond flour and cumin; cook for 1 minute. Then beat in stock and simmer for 2 minutes until thickened.

3. Add almond butter, almond milk, salt, and pepper. Simmer for 10 minutes until flavors are blended.

4. In small bowl combine almonds with Kale Pesto and mix. Serve soup with this mixture for topping.

Mushroom and Onion Soup

This soup serves as an excellent light lunch or as an appetizer before dinner.

INGREDIENTS | SERVES 6

6½ cups Roasted Vegetable Stock (see recipe in this chapter)

3 cups peeled, thinly sliced onions

2 cups sliced fresh mushrooms

1½ cups thinly sliced leeks

½ cup chopped shallots or green onions

1 teaspoon maple syrup

½ teaspoon ground black pepper

Combine all ingredients in a 6-quart slow cooker. Cover and cook on low 6–8 hours.

Gazpacho

Gazpacho is best made the day before so that the flavors will penetrate all the vegetables.

INGREDIENTS | SERVES 6

1 (28-ounce) can chopped tomatoes

1 medium green bell pepper, seeded and chopped

3 medium tomatoes, peeled and chopped

1 large cucumber, peeled and chopped

1 small onion, peeled and chopped

2 tablespoons olive oil

½ teaspoon ground black pepper

½ teaspoon paprika

¼ teaspoon cayenne pepper

1 teaspoon chopped chives

2 teaspoons chopped parsley

½ clove garlic, peeled and minced

4½ teaspoons lemon juice

1. Blend tomatoes in blender until smooth. Pour into large bowl. Add remaining ingredients to bowl and stir to combine.

2. Refrigerate at least 12 hours. Serve chilled.

Curried Cauliflower Soup

Orange cauliflower is an excellent variety to use in this recipe. It has 25 percent more vitamin A than white cauliflower and lends an attractive color to the soup.

INGREDIENTS | SERVES 4

1 pound cauliflower florets
2½ cups water
1 medium onion, peeled and minced
2 cloves garlic, peeled and minced
3 teaspoons curry powder
¼ teaspoon cumin

1. Place all ingredients in a 4-quart slow cooker. Stir. Cook on low for 8 hours.

2. Use an immersion blender to purée the soup or blend the soup in batches in a blender until smooth.

Curry Powder Power

Curry powder is a mixture of spices commonly used in South Asian cooking. While it does not correlate directly to any particular kind of curry, it is popular in Europe and North America to add an Indian flair to dishes. It can contain any number of spices, but nearly always includes turmeric, which gives it its distinctive yellow color.

Acorn Squash Autumn Bisque

This soup is a seasonally delicious taste of fall. The yellow-orange color of the squash is derived from its rich content of vitamin A. One cup of acorn squash provides more than 100 percent of the recommended daily amount of vitamin A.

INGREDIENTS | SERVES 6

2 cups Roasted Vegetable Stock (see recipe this chapter)

2 medium acorn squash, peeled, seeded, and cut into cubes

½ cup peeled, chopped onion

½ teaspoon ground cinnamon

¼ teaspoon ground coriander

¼ teaspoon ground cumin

½ cup unsweetened coconut milk

1 tablespoon lemon juice

1 teaspoon ground black pepper

1. Combine stock, squash, onion, cinnamon, coriander, and cumin in a 4-quart slow cooker. Cover and cook on high for 3–4 hours.

2. Blend squash mixture, coconut milk, and lemon juice in a food processor until smooth.

3. Season with pepper before serving.

Butternut Squash Soup

This soup is a scrumptious treat on a cool fall day. Warm family and friends with a delightful blend of aroma and flavor.

INGREDIENTS | SERVES 4

1 tablespoon olive oil

1 medium onion, peeled and chopped

1 pound butternut squash, peeled, seeded, and chopped

½ cup ground flaxseed

32 ounces Basic Vegetable Stock or Roasted Vegetable Stock (see recipes in this chapter)

1 cup almond milk

½ teaspoon ground cinnamon

¼ teaspoon ground cloves

¼ teaspoon ground nutmeg

1. In a soup pot or Dutch oven, heat olive oil over medium-high heat. Sauté onion and butternut squash in oil for 5 minutes.

2. Add ground flaxseed and stock and bring to a boil over high heat. Reduce heat to low and simmer for 45 minutes.

3. In batches, purée squash mixture in blender or food processor and return to pot.

4. Stir in almond milk, cinnamon, cloves, and nutmeg.

Pumpkin Soup

This is a perfect autumn soup to celebrate the harvest season. If you're short on time or pumpkins are out of season, substitute a 15-ounce can of puréed pumpkin (not pumpkin pie filling) for the fresh pumpkin.

INGREDIENTS | SERVES 6

1 medium sugar pumpkin, peeled, seeded, and chopped (reserve seeds)

3 medium leeks, sliced

1½ teaspoons minced fresh ginger

2 tablespoons olive oil, divided

½ teaspoon grated lemon zest

1 teaspoon lemon juice

2 quarts Basic Vegetable Stock (see recipe in this chapter) or low-sodium canned vegetable stock

1 teaspoon ground black pepper

Zesting

If you don't have a zester, you can still easily make lemon zest. Simply use your cheese grater, but be careful to grate only the rind and not the white pith, which tends to be bitter.

1. Preheat oven to 375°F.

2. Clean pumpkin seeds thoroughly, place them on a baking sheet, and sprinkle with salt to taste. Roast for approximately 5–8 minutes, until light golden. Remove from oven and set aside.

3. Place chopped pumpkin in a baking dish with leeks, ginger, and 1 tablespoon olive oil; roast for 45 minutes or until tender.

4. Transfer the cooked pumpkin mixture to a large stockpot and add zest, juice, stock, and pepper. Bring to a boil over medium-high heat. Reduce heat to low and simmer for 30–45 minutes.

5. To serve, ladle into serving bowls. Drizzle with remaining olive oil and sprinkle with toasted pumpkin seeds.

Sweet Potato Soup

*This luscious soup is a perfect winter treat. And it's a great post-workout snack.
It provides both fluid and carbohydrates to help refuel and rehydrate.*

INGREDIENTS | SERVES 4

3 large sweet potatoes, peeled and cubed

2 cups Roasted Vegetable Stock (see recipe in this chapter)

1 (15-ounce) can sliced mangoes, undrained

¼ teaspoon ground allspice

½ cup coconut milk

1. Place all ingredients except coconut milk in a 4-quart slow cooker. Cover and cook on low for 8 hours or on high for 4 hours.

2. When sweet potatoes are soft, purée soup in blender and stir in coconut milk.

Root Vegetable Soup

Red, white, and russet potatoes may be forbidden on the Paleo diet, but that doesn't mean all root vegetables are taboo. Parsnips, turnips, carrots, onions, and rutabagas are all fine, as are sweet potatoes in moderation. Enjoy this hearty soup with a spinach salad.

INGREDIENTS | SERVES 6

¼ cup olive oil

2 medium onions, peeled and chopped

6 cloves garlic, peeled and minced

1 small butternut squash, peeled, seeded, and cubed

3 large carrots, peeled and sliced

1 medium rutabaga, peeled and chopped

5 cups Basic Vegetable Stock (see recipe in this chapter)

1 teaspoon dried marjoram leaves

1 teaspoon dried thyme leaves

1 teaspoon salt

¼ teaspoon ground black pepper

1. In large soup pot or Dutch oven, heat olive oil over medium heat. Add onions and garlic; cook and stir for 4 minutes.

2. Add squash, carrots, and rutabaga; cook and stir for about 10 minutes or until vegetables start to brown.

3. Add stock, marjoram, thyme, salt, and pepper and bring to a simmer. Reduce heat to low, cover, and simmer for 45–55 minutes or until vegetables are tender. Correct seasoning if needed, and serve.

African Soup

Feel free to play around with the seasonings in this unique soup. A small pinch of curry powder would be an excellent addition.

INGREDIENTS | SERVES 6

2 tablespoons olive oil

2 medium onions, peeled and chopped

2 large red bell peppers, seeded and chopped

4 cloves garlic, peeled and minced

1 (28-ounce) can crushed tomatoes, with liquid

8 cups Roasted Vegetable Stock (see recipe in this chapter)

¼ teaspoon ground black pepper

¼ teaspoon chili powder

⅔ cup natural almond or cashew butter

½ cup chopped fresh cilantro

Nut Allergies and Intolerances

Nut allergies are very serious and can be life threatening. If you have a child or family member who has nut allergies, use sunflower butter in this recipe instead.

1. Heat olive oil in a large skillet over medium-high heat. Cook onions and bell peppers until softened, usually 3–4 minutes.

2. Add garlic and cook for 1 minute more, stirring constantly. Add cooked vegetables to a greased (coconut oil) 6-quart slow cooker.

3. Add tomatoes and their liquid, stock, pepper, and chili powder to the slow cooker. Cover and cook on high for 4 hours or on low for 8 hours.

4. One hour prior to serving stir in almond butter. Heat for an additional 45–60 minutes, until soup has been completely warmed through. Garnish with cilantro.

Garlicky Vegetable Soup

Garlic is a versatile vegetable with multiple health benefits, such as its blood pressure and cholesterol-lowering capabilities, as well as a high antioxidant profile, which aids in reducing inflammation and lowering the risk of developing diseases like cancer.

INGREDIENTS | SERVES 4

5 medium heads garlic, peeled (each clove peeled)

6 cups Roasted Vegetable Stock (see recipe in this chapter)

1 (6-ounce) can tomato paste

1 large yellow onion, peeled and diced

¼ teaspoon lemon juice

2 tablespoons olive oil

2 tablespoons chopped basil

1. Place all ingredients except oil and basil into a 4–6-quart slow cooker. Stir.

2. Cover and cook on low for 8 hours or on high for 5 hours.

3. Add olive oil. Use an immersion blender or blend soup in batches in a standard blender until smooth.

4. Garnish with basil and serve.

Cream of Carrot Soup with Coconut

This carrot soup will knock your socks off! The addition of coconut milk transforms an ordinary carrot and ginger soup into an unexpected treat.

INGREDIENTS | SERVES 6

3 medium carrots, peeled and chopped

1 medium sweet potato, peeled and chopped

1 medium yellow onion, peeled and chopped

3½ cups Basic Vegetable Stock (see recipe in this chapter)

3 cloves garlic, peeled and minced

2 teaspoons minced fresh ginger

1 (14-ounce) can coconut milk

1 teaspoon salt

¾ teaspoon cinnamon

1. In a large soup pot or stockpot over medium-high heat, bring carrots, sweet potato, and onion to a boil in stock. Add garlic and ginger, cover, reduce heat, and simmer for 20–25 minutes until carrots and potatoes are soft.

2. Allow to cool slightly, then transfer to a blender and purée until smooth.

3. Return soup to pot. Over very low heat, stir in coconut milk and salt, stirring well to combine. Heat just until heated through, another 3–4 minutes.

4. Garnish with cinnamon just before serving.

Cream of Cauliflower Soup

Blended cauliflower can be used as a thickener in recipes that normally call for potatoes or root vegetables. Best of all, cauliflower won't spike your insulin levels.

INGREDIENTS | SERVES 4

1 large head cauliflower, chopped

3 large stalks celery, chopped

1 medium carrot, peeled and chopped

2 cloves garlic, peeled and minced

1 medium onion, peeled and chopped

2 teaspoons ground cumin

½ teaspoon ground black pepper

1 tablespoon chopped parsley

¼ teaspoon dill

1. In a soup pot or Dutch oven, combine cauliflower, celery, carrot, garlic, onion, cumin, and pepper. Add water to just cover ingredients in pot. Bring to a boil over high heat.

2. Reduce heat to low. Simmer about 8 minutes or until vegetables are tender. Stir in parsley and dill before serving.

"Cream" of Mushroom Soup

This vegan- and Paleo-approved "cream" of mushroom soup is a simple and light main dish. It's also a perfect base to use when a recipe calls for canned cream soup.

INGREDIENTS | SERVES 4

2 tablespoons olive oil
2 tablespoons coconut butter
1 cup finely diced fresh mushrooms
4 tablespoons arrowroot powder
2 cups full-fat coconut milk
½ teaspoon ground black pepper

Cream Soup Variations

You can make any number of homemade cream soups with this recipe. If you would rather have cream of celery soup, use 1 cup finely diced celery instead of the mushrooms.

1. Heat oil and coconut butter in a deep saucepan over medium heat until sizzling. Add mushrooms and cook until soft, approximately 4–5 minutes.

2. In a medium bowl whisk arrowroot powder into coconut milk. Slowly add to mushrooms. Cook for 5–10 minutes, whisking constantly, until slightly thickened.

3. Carefully pour soup into a greased (coconut oil) 2½-quart slow cooker. Stir in pepper. Cook on high for 2 hours or on low for 4 hours.

"Cream" of Broccoli Soup

This "cream" soup serves as a light meal on its own, or can be poured over an entrée to enhance flavor and richness.

INGREDIENTS | SERVES 4

1 (12-ounce) bag frozen broccoli florets, thawed

1 small onion, peeled and diced

4 cups Basic Vegetable Stock (see recipe in this chapter)

½ teaspoon ground black pepper

1 cup (full-fat) coconut milk

1. Add broccoli, onion, stock, and pepper to a 2- or 4-quart slow cooker; cover and cook on low for 4 hours.

2. Use an immersion blender to purée the soup. Stir in coconut milk. Cover and cook on low, stirring occasionally, for 30 minutes or until the soup is heated through.

Caveman's Cabbage Soup

Slow-cooking cabbage soup preserves the nutrients in the cabbage and other vegetables, versus other, higher-temperature methods of preparation, which tend to destroy many of the nutrients.

INGREDIENTS | SERVES 14

1 small head cabbage, cored and chopped

2 green onions, chopped

1 medium red bell pepper, seeded and chopped

1 bunch celery, chopped

1 cup chopped carrots

4 cups Basic Vegetable Stock (see recipe in this chapter)

4 cups water

3 cloves garlic, peeled and minced

¼ teaspoon crushed red pepper flakes

¼ teaspoon dried basil

¼ teaspoon dried oregano

¼ teaspoon dried thyme

¼ teaspoon onion powder

1. Place cabbage, onions, bell pepper, celery, and carrots in a 6-quart slow cooker.

2. Pour in stock and water.

3. Stir in garlic, pepper flakes, basil, oregano, thyme, and onion powder. Cover and cook on low for 8–10 hours.

CHAPTER 7

Dinner Entrées

Veggie Kebabs with Chimichurri Sauce

Use whatever vegetables you have on hand for these tasty kebabs. Just remember to use vegetables that have about the same cooking time, or precook the harder produce so everything will grill to tender perfection at once.

INGREDIENTS | SERVES 4

1 medium red bell pepper, seeded and cut into large chunks

1 medium yellow bell pepper, seeded and cut into large chunks

1 medium red onion, peeled and cut into eighths

16 large button mushrooms

1 large yellow squash, cut into chunks

2 tablespoons olive oil

⅓ cup Chimichurri Sauce (see recipe in Chapter 12)

1. If using bamboo skewers, soak in cool water for 30 minutes to prevent burning.

2. Thread vegetables onto bamboo or metal skewers, alternating the produce. Brush with olive oil.

3. Grill 6" from medium coals, turning frequently, until vegetables are slightly charred on the edges and tender. Brush with Chimichurri Sauce, grill for 1 more minute, then serve.

Mushrooms and Greens

There are many types of exotic mushrooms available in the market now that weren't available even ten years ago. Take some time to browse through the selection and try some mushrooms you haven't tried before.

INGREDIENTS | SERVES 4

3 tablespoons olive oil

1 tablespoon avocado oil

2 medium shallots, peeled and minced

2 cloves garlic, peeled and minced

1 cup sliced cremini mushrooms

1 cup sliced chanterelle or oyster mushrooms

1 cup sliced shiitake mushrooms

2 cups chopped kale

1 cup chopped Swiss chard

¼ cup water

1 cup baby spinach leaves

2 tablespoons lemon juice

½ teaspoon salt

⅛ teaspoon ground black pepper

1. In large skillet, heat olive oil and avocado oil over medium heat. Add shallots and garlic; cook and stir for 2 minutes.

2. Add mushrooms; cook and stir until mushrooms give up their liquid, the liquid evaporates, and they start to brown, about 8–10 minutes.

3. Add kale, Swiss chard, and water; cover and steam for 2 minutes. Remove cover, add spinach, lemon juice, salt, and pepper. Stir, cover, and steam for another 2–4 minutes or until greens are tender. Stir and serve immediately.

Baked Stuffed Artichokes

These are worth a bit of effort. You can make them in advance, then finish cooking just before serving.

INGREDIENTS | SERVES 4

2 large artichokes

¼ cup lemon juice

2 tablespoons avocado oil

2 cloves garlic, peeled and chopped

½ large sweet onion, peeled and chopped

1 cup almond meal

1 tablespoon minced lemon peel

4 tablespoons chopped fresh parsley

½ teaspoon freshly ground black pepper

2 cups chopped spinach

4 quarts plus ½ cup water, divided

Juice and rind of ½ lemon

½ teaspoon ground coriander

1. Remove any tough or brown outside leaves from the artichokes. Using a sharp knife, cut off artichoke tops, about ½" down. Slam artichokes against a countertop to loosen leaves. Cut in half, from top to stem, and remove the thistly choke with a spoon. Trim the stem end. Place in a bowl of cold water mixed with ¼ cup lemon juice; set aside.

2. Heat oil in a large skillet over medium heat. Add garlic and onion and sauté for 5 minutes, stirring. Add almond meal, lemon peel, parsley, and pepper. Cook 2 minutes. Add spinach and stir until wilted, about 1 minute. Remove from heat and set aside.

3. Boil artichokes in 4 quarts water with juice and rind of ½ lemon, and coriander for 18 minutes. Remove artichokes but reserve the cooking water. Place artichokes cut side up in a baking dish with ½ cup water on the bottom. Stuff each half with spinach mixture.

4. Preheat oven to 375°F. Drizzle stuffed artichokes with a bit of the cooking water and bake for 25 minutes until filling is browned on top. Serve.

Coconut Cauliflower Curry

To save time chopping, substitute a bag of mixed frozen vegetables or use some leftover cooked sweet potatoes in this tropical yellow curry recipe.

INGREDIENTS | SERVES 4

¾ cup Basic Vegetable Stock (see recipe in Chapter 6)

1 cup coconut milk

1½ cups chopped green beans

1 small head cauliflower, chopped

2 medium carrots, peeled and diced

2 teaspoons minced fresh ginger

3 cloves garlic, peeled and minced

2 teaspoons curry powder

½ teaspoon turmeric

1 tablespoon maple syrup

¼ teaspoon salt

¼ teaspoon nutmeg

1 cup diced pineapple

2 tablespoons chopped fresh cilantro

1. Whisk together vegetable stock and coconut milk in a large saucepan.

2. Add remaining ingredients except for pineapple and cilantro, stirring well to combine. Bring to a slow simmer over low heat, cover, and cook for 8–10 minutes, stirring occasionally. Add pineapple and heat for 2 more minutes.

3. Top with cilantro and serve hot.

Caveman Vegetable Roast

Roasting concentrates the flavors of the veggies and brings out their sweetness, and makes the vegetables very tender. Season them with just about any herb or spice.

INGREDIENTS | SERVES 6

1 medium onion, peeled and cut into eighths

12 cloves garlic, peeled

1 medium sweet potato, peeled and cubed

1 large parsnip, peeled and cubed

1 medium red bell pepper, seeded and cut into strips

1 medium yellow bell pepper, seeded and cut into strips

¼ cup olive oil

1 tablespoon apple cider vinegar

1 teaspoon dried thyme leaves

1 teaspoon salt

⅛ teaspoon ground black pepper

1. Preheat oven to 400°F. On a large rimmed baking sheet, combine all ingredients. Toss to coat.

2. Roast for 40–50 minutes or until vegetables are tender and browned on the edges, stirring every 15 minutes. Serve warm or cool.

Sweet Potato Pasta

Sweet potatoes can be turned into "pasta noodles" just as squash and zucchini can. The only real work with this recipe is getting the hard flesh cut into thin strips. You can do this by yourself with a knife, a vegetable peeler, or a spiralizer, or you could try using a mandoline to help. Slice the potatoes into thin slices with the mandoline, then cut into pasta-like strips with your knife. Also try this with butternut squash and pumpkin.

INGREDIENTS | SERVES 4

2 tablespoons olive oil

2 large sweet potatoes, peeled and cut into thin strips

½ teaspoon salt

¼ cup Basic Vegetable Stock (see recipe in Chapter 6)

1. Heat olive oil in a large saucepan over medium-high heat. Add sweet potatoes and salt; cook and stir until almost tender, about 4 minutes.

2. Add stock and bring to a simmer; simmer for 2–3 minutes or until "pasta" is tender. Serve immediately.

Shirataki Noodles with Mushrooms

Shirataki noodles are a Japanese product made from yams. They have almost no calories and almost no carbs. They don't require any cooking, but they should be rinsed with hot water to remove a fishy odor before eating. Their texture is best if they are dry-fried before serving. This rich mushroom sauce adds lots of flavor.

INGREDIENTS | SERVES 4

2 tablespoons sesame oil

1 (8-ounce) package sliced cremini mushrooms

3 cloves garlic, peeled and minced

2 tablespoons coconut aminos

1 cup Basic Vegetable Stock (see recipe in Chapter 6)

1 tablespoon lemon juice

¼ teaspoon ground white pepper

4 (7-ounce) packages shirataki noodles

2 tablespoons toasted sesame seeds

Coconut Aminos

Coconut aminos can be found in the health food section of many supermarkets as well as in vitamin shops.

1. In large saucepan, heat sesame oil over medium heat. Add mushrooms and garlic; cook and stir until mushrooms give up their liquid and liquid evaporates, about 7 minutes.

2. Add coconut aminos, stock, lemon juice, and pepper and simmer for 8 minutes.

3. Meanwhile, cook noodles in boiling water based on package instructions. When done, drain noodles and rinse with hot water; drain again.

4. Heat another skillet over medium-high heat and add noodles. Cook and stir until noodles are dry.

5. Place noodles in a serving bowl and pour mushroom sauce over all. Sprinkle with sesame seeds and serve immediately.

Shirataki Noodles with Pesto

Pesto is usually made with lots of Parmesan or Romano cheese. But you don't have to use cheese to make a satisfying pesto sauce. Most people won't even miss it, since the pine nuts have a silky quality that is a good substitute for the cheese. This recipe must be served at once while the noodles are still hot and the pesto is melting into them.

INGREDIENTS | SERVES 4

2 cups fresh basil leaves
2 cloves garlic, peeled and minced
½ cup pine nuts, toasted
⅓ cup olive oil
1 tablespoon lemon juice
½ teaspoon salt
⅛ teaspoon ground black pepper
12 ounces shirataki noodles

1. In food processor or with a mortar and pestle, combine basil, garlic, and pine nuts until finely chopped.

2. Add olive oil slowly with the processor running, or while working the mortar and pestle. Season with lemon juice, salt, and pepper.

3. Cook noodles in boiling water based on package instructions. When cooked, drain noodles and rinse with hot water.

4. Heat a large pan over medium-high heat. Add noodles and fry, stirring frequently, until warm and toasted.

5. Transfer noodles to serving bowl and add pesto. Toss to coat and serve immediately.

Roasted Tomato Zucchini Pasta

Roasting tomatoes concentrates their flavor and sweetness. Use Roma tomatoes for best results in this recipe. They are meatier and have less water and fewer seeds than beefsteak or other types of tomatoes.

INGREDIENTS | SERVES 4

2 large zucchini

14 medium Roma tomatoes, sliced

1 medium onion, peeled and chopped

2 cloves garlic, peeled and sliced

3 tablespoons olive oil, divided

½ teaspoon salt

⅛ teaspoon ground white pepper

1 tablespoon maple syrup

1 teaspoon dried oregano

½ teaspoon dried basil

½ teaspoon dried thyme

1. Cut zucchini into noodle-shaped strips using a sharp knife or a spiral cutter, avoiding the seed center. Set aside.

2. Preheat oven to 325°F. Place tomatoes on a rimmed baking sheet. Sprinkle with onion, garlic, 2 tablespoons olive oil, salt, and pepper. Drizzle with maple syrup.

3. Roast tomatoes for 1½ hours or until they start to break down and look brown around the edges.

4. In large saucepan, heat remaining 1 tablespoon olive oil. Sauté zucchini noodles for 2–3 minutes or until tender. Add tomatoes and all of the scrapings from the baking sheet used to roast the tomatoes along with oregano, basil, and thyme; cook and stir for 1 minute longer. Serve immediately.

Sweet Potato Pasta with Pumpkin Seed Pesto

Tender "pasta" made with sweet potatoes is combined with a nutty and crunchy pesto made with pumpkin seeds, basil, and parsley in this delicious recipe. It's colorful and very good for you.

INGREDIENTS | SERVES 4

1 cup pumpkin seeds

1 cup fresh basil leaves

⅓ cup flat-leaf parsley

¼ cup pine nuts

2 cloves garlic, peeled and minced

3 tablespoons lemon juice

½ teaspoon salt

⅛ teaspoon ground black pepper

7 tablespoons extra-virgin olive oil, divided

5 tablespoons water, divided

2 large sweet potatoes, peeled and cut into thin strips

1. In blender or food processor, combine pumpkin seeds, basil, parsley, pine nuts, and garlic. Blend or process until finely chopped.

2. With motor running, add lemon juice, salt, pepper, and 5 tablespoons olive oil to the blender or food processor. Process until a paste forms. Add up to 2 tablespoons water if needed to reach desired consistency. Place the pesto in a large serving bowl.

3. Heat remaining olive oil in a large skillet over medium heat. Add sweet potato strips; cook and stir until almost tender, about 4 minutes.

4. Add 3 tablespoons water and bring to a simmer. Simmer for 2–3 minutes or until the "pasta" is tender. Immediately pour over the pesto in the serving bowl and gently toss to coat. Serve immediately.

Paleo Spaghetti

Spaghetti squash is a great alternative to traditional pasta. Serve with your favorite sauce or pesto or toss it with a little olive oil for a simple side dish.

INGREDIENTS | SERVES 4

1 large spaghetti squash

Pasta Alternative

Spaghetti squash is a fantastic carbohydrate source for all you pasta addicts out there. This squash looks like spaghetti when the flesh is peeled from the skin. Its texture is similar to pasta, and most important, it's quite filling.

1. Preheat oven to 350°F.

2. Cut squash in half lengthwise. Place cut side down in a baking dish with ¼" water.

3. Bake 30 minutes, then turn cut side up and continue baking until soft, approximately 10 minutes.

4. Shred squash with a fork and serve.

Slow-Cooked Spaghetti Squash

Serve this as a replacement for pasta tossed with fresh herbs, pepper, and your favorite sauce.

INGREDIENTS | SERVES 1

2 cups water

1 medium spaghetti squash

1. With a skewer or large fork, puncture several holes in spaghetti squash.

2. Pour water into a 2-quart slow cooker and add the whole squash. Cover and cook on low for 8–9 hours.

3. Split squash and remove the seeds. Use a fork to shred the strands from the squash, which will resemble angel hair pasta.

Eggplant Steaks

Eggplant has a very meaty taste and texture when grilled. This unusual vegetable has to be salted before it is cooked or it will release too much moisture and will steam instead of grilling. Topping the eggplant with a sauce made from sun-dried tomatoes makes this a very appealing meal.

INGREDIENTS | SERVES 4

2 large eggplants, cut into ¾"-thick slices

1 tablespoon salt

1 cup hot water

6 sun-dried tomatoes (not packed in oil)

¼ cup olive oil

⅓ cup almond meal

1 tablespoon lemon juice

2 teaspoons fresh thyme leaves

Pinch salt

⅛ teaspoon ground white pepper

3 tablespoons olive oil

1. Place eggplant slices on a baking sheet and sprinkle with 1 tablespoon salt. Let stand for 1 hour.

2. Rinse eggplant thoroughly under cool running water. Place between kitchen towels and press down to remove moisture.

3. Combine hot water and sun-dried tomatoes in small bowl; let stand for 15 minutes to rehydrate. Remove tomatoes from water and coarsely chop.

4. In food processor or blender, combine ¼ cup olive oil, tomatoes, almonds, lemon juice, thyme, pinch salt, and pepper. Blend until combined.

5. Prepare and preheat grill. Brush eggplant with 3 tablespoons olive oil and place on grill rack over medium coals. Grill for 6–8 minutes, turning once, until eggplant slices are tender with nice grill marks. Top each with a spoonful of tomato mixture and serve immediately.

Ratatouille

Ratatouille is simply a rich and hearty vegetable stew. You can use any of your favorite veggies in this easy recipe. The colors, flavors, and textures in this dish really highlight produce, whether you're making it in the summer or winter. Serve with some toasted Paleo Sandwich Bread (see recipe in Chapter 3).

INGREDIENTS | SERVES 4

3 tablespoons olive oil

1 medium onion, peeled and chopped

4 cloves garlic, peeled and minced

1 medium eggplant, peeled and cubed

1 medium red bell pepper, seeded and chopped

1 cup sliced cremini mushrooms

1 cup chopped zucchini

1 cup chopped and seeded tomatoes

½ teaspoon salt

⅛ teaspoon ground black pepper

⅓ cup chopped fresh basil

2 tablespoons chopped fresh parsley

1. Heat olive oil in large skillet over medium heat. Add onion and garlic; cook and stir for 3 minutes. Add eggplant; cook and stir for 5–6 minutes or until eggplant is almost soft.

2. Add bell pepper, mushrooms, and zucchini. Cook and stir for another 2–3 minutes. Add tomatoes, salt, and pepper and bring to a simmer.

3. Simmer for 7–9 minutes or until everything is blended. Sprinkle with basil and parsley and serve immediately.

Summer-Style Chili

This light chili is full of summer vegetables. It's a very low-calorie,
high-fiber chili loaded with vitamins and minerals.

INGREDIENTS | SERVES 8

1 medium bulb fennel, diced
4 medium radishes, diced
2 stalks celery, diced, including leaves
2 large carrots, peeled and cut into coin-sized pieces
1 medium onion, peeled and diced
1 medium shallot, peeled and diced
4 cloves garlic, peeled and sliced
1 small habanero pepper, seeded and diced
12 ounces tomato paste
½ teaspoon dried oregano
½ teaspoon ground black pepper
½ teaspoon crushed rosemary
½ teaspoon cayenne
½ teaspoon ground chipotle
1 teaspoon chili powder
1 teaspoon tarragon
¼ teaspoon cumin
¼ teaspoon celery seed
2 medium zucchini, cubed
2 medium summer squash, cubed
10 Campari tomatoes, quartered

1. In a 4-quart slow cooker add all ingredients except zucchini, summer squash, and tomatoes. Stir.

2. Cook on low for 6–7 hours; then stir in zucchini, summer squash, and tomatoes. Cook on high for an additional 30 minutes. Stir before serving.

Spiced "Baked" Eggplant

Serve this as a main dish over a garden salad, or as a side dish, as is.

INGREDIENTS | SERVES 4

1 pound cubed eggplant

⅓ cup peeled, sliced onion

½ teaspoon red pepper flakes

½ teaspoon crushed rosemary

¼ cup lemon juice

Place all ingredients in a 1½–2-quart slow cooker. Cook on low for 3 hours or until eggplant is tender.

Cold Snap

Take care not to put a cold ceramic slow cooker insert directly into a heated slow cooker. The sudden shift in temperature can cause it to crack. If you want to prepare your ingredients the night before use, refrigerate them in reusable containers, not in the insert.

Zucchini Casserole

This highly nutritious and delicious vegetable compilation is the perfect lunchtime portion.

INGREDIENTS | SERVES 2

4 medium zucchini, sliced

1 large red onion, peeled and sliced

1 medium green bell pepper, seeded and cut into thin strips

1 (16-ounce) can diced tomatoes, undrained

1 teaspoon lemon juice

½ teaspoon ground black pepper

½ teaspoon basil

1 tablespoon olive oil

1. Combine all ingredients except olive oil in a 2-quart slow cooker. Cook on low for 3 hours.

2. Drizzle casserole with olive oil. Cook on low for 1½ hours more.

Acorn Squash Casserole

Try this recipe using other seasonal fall vegetables like butternut squash or eggplant. Round out this classic comfort cuisine and serve with Pumpkin Soup or Sweet Potato Soup (see recipes in Chapter 6).

INGREDIENTS | SERVES 6

2 medium acorn squash, peeled, seeded, and sliced

1 small red onion, peeled and sliced

1 medium green bell pepper, seeded and cut into strips

2 cups diced fresh tomatoes

1 teaspoon lemon juice

½ teaspoon ground black pepper

½ teaspoon basil

1 tablespoon coconut oil, melted

1. Combine all ingredients except coconut oil in a 2-quart slow cooker.

2. Cover and cook on low for 3 hours.

3. Drizzle casserole with coconut oil and cook another 1½ hours on low.

Slow-Cooked Paleo Stuffed Portobello

Portobello mushrooms are a rich source of antioxidants, all of which are generally preserved through cooking, unlike other vegetables, whose phytonutrient compounds are often destroyed during the cooking process.

INGREDIENTS | SERVES 2

4 large portobello mushrooms, stems removed and chopped, centers removed

1½ cups chopped cherry tomatoes

¼ cup arrowroot powder

3 tablespoons olive oil

¼ cup lime juice

1 tablespoon dried basil

½ teaspoon lemon juice

½ teaspoon ground black pepper

1. Place mushroom centers and stems, tomatoes, arrowroot powder, olive oil, lime juice, basil, lemon juice, and pepper in a large mixing bowl. Mix well.

2. Place mushroom caps on bottom of a greased (with coconut oil) 6-quart oval slow cooker. Spoon mushroom and tomato mixture on top of mushrooms. Cover and cook on low for 4–7 hours.

Spaghetti Squash and Garden Vegetables

Spaghetti squash is rich in B vitamins and also promotes proper cellular function.

INGREDIENTS | SERVES 2

1 medium spaghetti squash
1–2 cups water
2 tablespoons olive oil
1 large onion, peeled and diced
2 cloves garlic, peeled and minced
5 Roma tomatoes, chopped
3 tablespoons chopped fresh basil
½ teaspoon ground black pepper

1. Pierce spaghetti squash several times with a fork. Place it in a 4–6-quart slow cooker and cover with 1–2 cups of water.

2. Cover and cook on low for 6–8 hours or high for 3–4 hours. Remove from slow cooker and let it cool. Drain water from the slow cooker.

3. While squash is cooling, heat oil in a large nonstick skillet over medium-high heat. Sauté onion for 5–10 minutes until tender. Add garlic, stir, and turn off heat.

4. Slice cooked squash in half, seed it, and use a fork to shred the strands from the squash. Return strands to the slow cooker. Add onion, garlic, and oil mixture to the slow cooker. Add tomatoes and toss so that they become warm.

5. Add basil and toss. Sprinkle with pepper and serve warm.

Vegetable Fajita Filling

*Use large lettuce or cabbage leaves as the fajita "wrap," or
serve over a starchy or seasonal root vegetable.*

INGREDIENTS | SERVES 3

3 large onions, peeled and thinly sliced

1 large red bell pepper, seeded and
thinly sliced

1 large green bell pepper, seeded and
thinly sliced

2 tablespoons olive oil

½ teaspoon paprika

½ teaspoon ground black pepper

Place all ingredients in a 4–6-quart slow cooker and toss well. Cover and cook on high for 3½–4 hours.

Leek, Turnip, and Carrot Potage

Potage is a classic French homestyle soup that is perfect for a blustery winter day.

INGREDIENTS | SERVES 6

4 cups sliced leeks

4 medium turnips, peeled and cubed

2 large carrots, peeled and diced

5 cups water

½ teaspoon ground white pepper

1. Place all ingredients in a 4-quart slow cooker. Cook on low for 7 hours.

2. Purée using an immersion blender, or purée in batches in a blender. Serve piping hot.

Sweet Potato Gratin with Leeks and Onions

The combination of sweet and savory makes this a fascinating, unique, and delicious dish.

INGREDIENTS | SERVES 6

4 tablespoons olive oil

2 large leeks, white parts only, rinsed and chopped

2 large sweet onions, peeled and finely chopped

2 stalks celery with tops, finely chopped

4 medium sweet potatoes, peeled and thinly sliced

1 teaspoon dried thyme

½ teaspoon ground black pepper

3 cups coconut milk

1½ cups arrowroot powder

2 tablespoons coconut butter, cut in small pieces

1. Heat olive oil in a skillet over medium heat. Sauté leeks, onions, and celery for 3–5 minutes until softened.

2. Grease a 4-quart slow cooker with coconut oil.

3. Layer sweet potato slices in the slow cooker with the sautéed vegetables. Sprinkle thyme and pepper on each layer as you go along. Finish with a layer of potatoes.

4. Add coconut milk until it meets the top layer of potatoes. Then add arrowroot powder. Dot with coconut butter.

5. Cover and cook on high for 4 hours, on low for 8 hours, or until potatoes are fork tender. In the last hour of cooking, vent the lid of the slow cooker with a chopstick or wooden spoon handle to allow excess condensation to escape.

Curried Sunchokes, Plantain, and Apples

Sunchokes and plantains do not make frequent appearances at the American table, but here they make a gentle trio with the all-American apple adding its own sweetness. With the addition of curry and ginger, this simple dish becomes an international star.

INGREDIENTS | SERVES 2

3 tablespoons olive oil

1 medium onion, peeled and thinly sliced

2–3 tablespoons grated fresh ginger

4 cloves garlic, peeled and lightly crushed

2 teaspoons ground turmeric

1 teaspoon curry powder

1 pound sunchokes (Jerusalem artichokes), scrubbed and thinly sliced

1 large cooking apple, cored and thinly sliced

1 medium yellow plantain, peeled and thinly sliced

1 cup Basic Vegetable Stock (see recipe in Chapter 6)

1. Heat oil in a large skillet over medium heat. Add onion, ginger, and garlic and sauté for 2–3 minutes. Stir in turmeric and curry powder and cook 2–3 minutes more. Add sunchokes, apple, and plantain and stir until mixture is coated with seasoning.

2. Stir in vegetable stock, reduce heat to medium-low, and cover. Cook for about 10 minutes more or until sunchokes are just tender.

About Sunchokes

Native to North America and once a staple for some Native American tribes, the sunchoke—also called a Jerusalem artichoke—is not really an artichoke but instead a tuber from the sunflower family; it resembles an oddly shaped small potato. Its crunchy texture resembles that of water chestnuts. Sunchokes may be cooked or eaten raw.

CHAPTER 8

Healthy Snacks

Nut Butter Spread

This is a delicious alternative to peanut butter or mayonnaise when making a sandwich or a salad dressing. For the best flavor, roast the nuts before you process them. Add anything you wish to this basic recipe, including melted dark chocolate for a homemade version of Nutella, vanilla for more flavor, or spices such as cinnamon or cardamom for variety. Cover and refrigerate for up to a week.

INGREDIENTS | MAKES 1 CUP

2 cups pecans, almonds, or hazelnuts
Pinch sea salt

1. To toast nuts, place in a single layer on a rimmed baking sheet. Roast in a preheated 400°F oven for 15–20 minutes or until nuts are fragrant and light golden. Let nuts cool before you process them.

2. Place nuts in a heavy-duty food processor or blender. Cover and process for 5–10 minutes or until the nut butter is desired consistency. Season with salt.

Almond Butter

Make almond butter "sandwiches" with frozen banana slices or apple slices. Spread almond butter and Strawberry Jelly (see recipe in Chapter 11) between two fruit slices for a quick and satisfying snack.

INGREDIENTS | MAKES 16 OUNCES

2 cups almonds

Olive oil, as needed (about 2–3 teaspoons)

1. Place almonds in food processor and turn on.

2. Add olive oil as needed, depending on creaminess desired.

Tropical Cashew Nut Butter

You can make a homemade cashew nut butter with a variety of oils including coconut oil, olive oil, and avocado oil, so feel free to substitute whatever you have on hand. You're in for a real treat, though, if you use coconut oil in this recipe!

INGREDIENTS | MAKES ¾ CUP

2 cups roasted cashews

1½ teaspoons maple syrup

¼ teaspoon salt

3–4 tablespoons coconut oil

1. Process cashews, maple syrup, and salt in a food processor on high speed until cashews form a thick paste.

2. Slowly add coconut oil until mixture is smooth and creamy, scraping down sides and adding a little more oil as needed.

Making Nut Butters

Nut butters can be very expensive to purchase but are so easy to make at home! Try making almond, walnut, or macadamia nut butter for a delicious alternative to peanut butter. Roasted nuts work best. Just place them on a baking sheet and roast in a preheated 400°F oven for 6–8 minutes or toast them on the stovetop in a dry skillet for a few minutes.

Vegan Chocolate Hazelnut Spread

Treat yourself or your family with this rich, sticky chocolate spread. This one will have you dancing around the kitchen and licking your spoons!

INGREDIENTS | MAKES 1 CUP

2 cups chopped hazelnuts
½ cup unsweetened cocoa powder
¾ cup maple syrup
½ teaspoon vanilla
4–5 tablespoons avocado oil

1. Process hazelnuts in a food processor until very finely ground, about 3–4 minutes.

2. Add cocoa powder, maple syrup, and vanilla, and process to combine.

3. Add oil a little bit at a time until mixture is soft and creamy and desired consistency is reached. You may need to add a bit more or less than 4–5 tablespoons.

Homemade Nut Milk

Homemade nut milk is delicious in breakfast cereal, oatmeal, and smoothies, and it's also great to use in baking. If you don't have a sieve or cheesecloth, you can still enjoy this recipe, but it will be a bit grainy.

INGREDIENTS | MAKES 4 CUPS

1 cup raw almonds or cashews
Water for soaking
4 cups water
½ teaspoon salt
½ teaspoon vanilla

Does It Taste Different from What You Expected?

If you read the label of most commercially available nondairy milks, you'll find them loaded with sugar! If you like a sweeter taste, try adding some maple syrup, stevia, or coconut sugar to this recipe.

1. In a large bowl, cover nuts with plenty of water and allow to soak for at least 1 hour or overnight. Drain.

2. Blend soaked nuts with 4 cups water in a food processor. Purée on high until smooth.

3. Strain through cheesecloth or a sieve.

4. Stir in salt and vanilla.

Fried Zucchini Sticks

You don't have to deep-fry these zucchini sticks; just sauté them in a bit of olive oil if you prefer. This is a great appetizer or snack for kids!

INGREDIENTS | SERVES 4

¾ cup almond flour
½ teaspoon garlic powder
¾ teaspoon Italian seasoning
¼ teaspoon salt
4 medium zucchini, cut into strips
4 tablespoons olive oil

1. In a large bowl or pan, combine almond flour, garlic powder, Italian seasoning, and salt.

2. Lightly toss zucchini strips with flour mixture, coating well.

3. Heat oil in a large skillet or frying pan over medium-high heat. When oil is hot, gently add zucchini strips to pan.

4. Fry until light golden brown on all sides, about 8 minutes. Drain on paper towels. Serve warm.

Curried Kale Chips

Kale contains powerful antioxidants, including at least forty different flavonoids, which fight cancer and can help reduce inflammation in your body. The leafy green is also a fabulous source of fiber. And curry powder is made with turmeric, which contains curcumin, a compound that helps reduce the risk of cancer. But the best thing about this combination is that it tastes wonderful!

INGREDIENTS | SERVES 6

2 bunches kale
2 tablespoons extra-virgin olive oil
1 tablespoon coconut oil, melted
2 tablespoons curry powder
1 teaspoon ground ginger
½ teaspoon ground cardamom
¼ teaspoon cayenne pepper
1 teaspoon salt

1. Preheat oven to 350°F. Wash kale well and dry thoroughly. Cut out any large ribs and discard. Cut kale leaves into 3" pieces.

2. In a small bowl, combine olive oil and coconut oil and mix well. Stir in curry powder, ginger, cardamom, and cayenne pepper and mix until combined.

3. Pour curry mixture over kale leaves and massage with your hands until the leaves are coated. Arrange leaves in a single layer on two baking sheets. Bake for 15–18 minutes, rotating pans after 10 minutes. The kale will not be crisp.

4. Remove from oven and sprinkle with salt. Let stand until leaves are crisp. Store at room temperature in airtight container.

No-Sugar Apricot Applesauce

You don't really need to peel the apples if you're short on time, but it only takes about 5 minutes and will give you a smoother sauce. Try adding a touch of nutmeg or pumpkin pie spice for extra flavor.

INGREDIENTS | MAKES 4 CUPS

6 medium apples, peeled, cored, and chopped

⅓ cup water

½ cup chopped dried apricots

4 large pitted dates, chopped

¼ teaspoon ground cinnamon

1. Add apples and water to a large soup pot or stockpot and bring to a low boil over medium-high heat. Reduce heat to low, cover, and simmer for 15 minutes, stirring occasionally.

2. Add apricots and dates and simmer for another 10–15 minutes.

3. Mash with a large fork until desired consistency is reached, or allow to cool slightly and purée in a blender until smooth.

4. Sprinkle with cinnamon before serving.

Chocolate Nut Bars

Make sure you u e good-quality chocolate with as few ingredients as possible. You don't want to eat polyglycerol polyricinoleate (PGPR), which is a new, cheap additive that corporations are adding to chocolate in place of cocoa butter. Good dark chocolate should have just a few ingredients and should be at least 70 percent cacao.

INGREDIENTS | SERVES 12

1 cup hazelnuts

1 cup walnuts

1½ cups pecans

1 pound dark chocolate, cut into small pieces

1. Preheat oven to 350°F. Place hazelnuts, walnuts, and pecans on a baking sheet. Bake for 10–15 minutes or just until nuts are fragrant and start to brown. Remove from oven and cool completely.

2. Coarsely chop nuts and place on a parchment paper–lined baking sheet.

3. Reserve ⅓ cup chocolate; place the remaining chocolate in a heavy saucepan over low heat. Melt, stirring occasionally, until mixture is smooth. Remove from heat and stir in reserved chocolate until melted; this tempers the chocolate so it will stay solid at room temperature.

4. Pour chocolate over nuts to coat. Let stand until set, then break into bars. Store in airtight container at room temperature.

Watermelon Pops

Frozen pops are the quintessential frozen summer treats. For this recipe you can freeze servings of the sweet puréed mixture in muffin cups, paper cups, or molds you buy at specialty stores. You will need flat sticks to serve as handles for your homemade creations. Vary the fruit used in this recipe to suit your own tastes, and enjoy a refreshing and easy treat!

INGREDIENTS | MAKES 8 POPS

2 cups cubed seedless watermelon

½ cup coconut milk

1 tablespoon lime juice

1 tablespoon maple syrup

1. Combine all ingredients in blender or food processor and blend or process until smooth.

2. Pour into frozen-pop molds and insert sticks. If using paper cups or muffin tins, freeze for about an hour, then insert sticks. Cover and freeze until firm, about 5–7 hours. Unmold to serve.

"Graham" Crackers

It's hard to believe that you can make graham-like crackers that are Paleo acceptable. But the explosion in gluten-free products and flours means you can make this childhood treat without any type of wheat or grain. Coconut and hazelnut flours are naturally sweet, and this cracker has a mild, nutty taste.

INGREDIENTS | MAKES 30–36 CRACKERS

1 cup hazelnut flour

¾ cup coconut flour

¼ cup tapioca starch

¼ teaspoon baking soda

½ teaspoon cream of tartar

2 teaspoons cinnamon

¼ teaspoon salt

⅓ cup maple syrup

3 tablespoons coconut oil

¼ cup coconut milk

1 tablespoon water

2 teaspoons vanilla

1. Preheat oven to 350°F. In large bowl, combine hazelnut flour, coconut flour, tapioca starch, baking soda, cream of tartar, cinnamon, and salt, and mix until one color.

2. In small saucepan, combine maple syrup, coconut oil, coconut milk, and water and heat until oil melts.

3. Add coconut milk mixture to dry ingredients along with vanilla and mix until dough forms. You may need to add more of either of the flours or more water for the right consistency (it should be dough-like). Wrap in plastic wrap and refrigerate for 1 hour.

4. Line a baking sheet with parchment paper. Roll dough into 2" balls and place on lined baking sheet about 3" apart. Top with another sheet of parchment paper and flatten balls using a rolling pin to ⅛" thickness. Carefully peel off the top piece of paper. Prick the dough with a fork.

5. Bake for 12–15 minutes or until crackers are set and golden brown. Cool on wire racks. Store in airtight container at room temperature.

Cinnamon Pumpkin Seeds

When you carve pumpkins for Halloween, always save the seeds for this recipe. The only trick is to separate the seeds from the fibers. Put the seeds and fibers in a large bowl, cover with water, and let stand for about 10 minutes. The seeds will start to float. Then work with your hands to remove the seeds from the stringy part. Discard the stringy part, pat the seeds dry, and begin.

INGREDIENTS | MAKES 2 CUPS

2 cups pumpkin seeds

1 tablespoon coconut oil, melted

2 tablespoons coconut sugar

2 teaspoons cinnamon

½ teaspoon salt

¼ teaspoon nutmeg

1. Preheat oven to 325°F. Place pumpkin seeds on a rimmed baking sheet. Drizzle with coconut oil and stir to coat. Spread into a single layer. Sprinkle with coconut sugar.

2. Roast for 18–23 minutes, stirring once during cooking, until seeds are light golden brown. Sprinkle with cinnamon, salt, and nutmeg and toss to coat. Cool completely before storing in an airtight container for up to 1 week.

Curried Nuts and Fruit

You can buy good-quality curry powder at any grocery store, or make your own. It is usually made from cinnamon, turmeric, cumin, mustard and fennel seeds, pepper, nutmeg, cardamom, ginger, and cayenne pepper, among other spices. It's delicious when combined with crunchy nuts and tart dried fruit in this easy recipe.

INGREDIENTS | MAKES 4 CUPS

1 cup broken walnuts

1 cup small whole pecans

2 tablespoons coconut oil

1 tablespoon extra-virgin olive oil

1 tablespoon curry powder

1 cup sunflower seeds

1 cup unsweetened dried cranberries

½ cup chopped dried unsulfured apricots

1. In medium bowl, combine walnuts and pecans; set aside.

2. In large saucepan, combine coconut oil and olive oil; melt over medium heat. Add curry powder; cook and stir for about 1 minute until fragrant.

3. Add walnuts and pecans to saucepan; cook, stirring frequently, until nuts are toasted and slightly crisp. Remove walnuts and pecans from heat and transfer nuts to bowl. Add sunflower seeds to pan and toast for 1–2 minutes. Add to bowl.

4. Stir in cranberries and apricots and toss to coat. Spread on paper towel and let cool. Store in an airtight container.

Roasted Spicy Pumpkin Seeds

These spicy seeds are sure to be a favorite with the family for snacking. They are quick to prepare and easy to grab for on-the-go snacks.

INGREDIENTS | SERVES 6

3 cups raw pumpkin seeds
½ cup olive oil
½ teaspoon garlic powder
½ teaspoon ground black pepper

Pumpkin Seed Benefits

Pumpkin seeds have great health benefits. They contain L-tryptophan, a compound found to naturally fight depression, and they are high in zinc, a mineral that protects against osteoporosis.

1. Preheat oven to 300°F.

2. In a medium bowl, mix together all ingredients until pumpkin seeds are evenly coated. Spread in an even layer on a baking sheet.

3. Bake for 1 hour and 15 minutes, stirring every 10–15 minutes.

Paleo Hummus

This is a great alternative to the traditional legume-based hummus.

INGREDIENTS | SERVES 8

4 medium beets, scrubbed, cooked, and cubed

¼ cup raw tahini paste

¼ cup lemon juice

1 small clove garlic, peeled and pressed

Place all ingredients in a food processor and pulse until smooth. Chill and serve.

Homemade Tomato Juice

This thirst-quencher is loaded with electrolytes to help you rehydrate and replenish after working out. It's an all-natural "energy drink"!

INGREDIENTS | SERVES 4

10 large tomatoes, seeded and sliced

1 teaspoon lemon juice

¼ teaspoon ground black pepper

1 tablespoon maple syrup

1. Place tomatoes in a 2-quart slow cooker. Cover; cook on low for 4–6 hours.

2. Press cooked tomatoes through a sieve. Add remaining ingredients and chill.

Lemonade

Serve cold on a hot summer day or warm on a cold winter's night!

INGREDIENTS | SERVES 6

5 cups water
¾ cup lemon juice
¾ cup maple syrup
1 (2") piece gingerroot, peeled and sliced

1. Combine all ingredients in a 2-quart or smaller slow cooker. Cover and cook on high for 2–3 hours (if mixture begins to boil, turn heat to low).

2. Turn to low to keep warm for serving, or chill and serve over ice. Remove gingerroot before serving.

Orangeade

This old-fashioned favorite is a thirst-quenching breakfast beverage.

INGREDIENTS | SERVES 6

5 cups water
Juice from 5 large oranges
¾ cup maple syrup
1 (2") piece gingerroot peeled and sliced

1. Combine all ingredients in a 2-quart slow cooker. Cover and cook on high for 2–3 hours (if mixture begins to boil, turn heat to low).

2. Allow to cool and serve chilled. Remove gingerroot before serving.

CHAPTER 9

Green Smoothies

Cucumber-Mint Smoothie

The light taste of cucumber and powerfully fragrant mint combine with deep green romaine in this smooth and refreshing smoothie. Not only can this be a great start to your day, it can also be the sweet end of it!

INGREDIENTS | MAKES 3–4 CUPS

1 cup chopped romaine lettuce

2 medium cucumbers, peeled and quartered

¼ cup chopped mint

1 cup water, divided

1. Place romaine, cucumbers, mint, and ½ cup water in a blender and combine thoroughly.

2. Add remaining water while blending until desired texture is achieved.

Cucumbers Aren't Just Water

Even though a cucumber is mostly water (and fiber), it is far more than a tasty, hydrating, and filling snack option. These green veggies are a great addition to a diet in need of moisture and clarity . . . for the skin! A clear complexion is an aesthetic benefit of consuming cucumbers.

Mango Berry Smoothie

Watercress acts as a beautiful background green for this deliciously sweet and smooth recipe. The mangoes, raspberries, and coconut milk provide a healthy serving of vitamins, minerals, and strong antioxidants.

INGREDIENTS | MAKES 3–4 CUPS

1 cup chopped watercress

2 medium mangoes, pitted and peeled

2 pints raspberries

1½ cups coconut milk, divided

Mangoes and Digestion

Mangoes aid in digestion by combating uncomfortable acids in the digestive system and creating a more placid, balanced system capable of a smooth, regular digestive process.

1. Place watercress, mangoes, raspberries, and ¾ cup coconut milk in a blender and blend until thoroughly combined.

2. Add remaining coconut milk while blending until desired texture is achieved.

Green Banana-Berry Smoothie

Satisfy your sweet tooth with a delicious blend of bananas, blueberries, and strawberries.

INGREDIENTS | MAKES 3–4 CUPS

1 cup romaine lettuce
2 medium bananas, peeled
1 pint strawberries
1 pint blueberries
2 cups almond milk, divided

1. Place romaine, bananas, berries, and 1 cup almond milk in a blender and blend until thoroughly combined.

2. Add remaining almond milk while blending until desired texture is achieved.

Peachy Orange Banana Smoothie

Delightfully refreshing citrus paired with sweet peaches and smooth bananas makes this a delicious treat for breakfast, lunch, a snack, or even dessert.

INGREDIENTS | MAKES 3–4 CUPS

1 cup chopped watercress
1 large orange, peeled
2 medium peaches, pitted
1 medium banana, peeled
1 cup coconut milk, divided

1. Place watercress, orange, peaches, banana, and ½ cup coconut milk in a blender and blend until thoroughly combined.

2. Add remaining coconut milk while blending until desired texture is achieved.

Sweet Greens Smoothie

Apples and spinach in the same smoothie may seem like an unlikely pair, but they work together well. Bananas add a touch of creaminess as well.

INGREDIENTS | MAKES 3–4 CUPS

1 cup spinach

2 medium bananas, peeled

2 medium apples, cored and peeled

2 cups almond milk, divided

1. Place spinach, bananas, apples, and 1 cup almond milk in a blender and blend until thoroughly combined.

2. Add remaining almond milk while blending until desired texture is achieved.

Fiber Benefits

Leafy greens, vegetables, and fruits all contain some amount of this miracle substance. Fiber-filled foods make your stomach feel full and help to clear your intestinal tract by remaining nearly intact throughout digestion. Although fiber is available in pill and powder forms, it's much better to get your fiber from spinach, broccoli, or fresh fruit.

Green Citrus Smoothie

Fight illness with this delicious blend of vitamins (lots of vitamin C!), minerals, fiber, and antioxidants.

INGREDIENTS | MAKES 3–4 CUPS

1 cup chopped watercress
1 large grapefruit, peeled
2 medium oranges, peeled
1 medium banana, peeled
1 cup water, divided

1. Place watercress, grapefruit, oranges, banana, and ½ cup water in a blender and blend until thoroughly combined.

2. Add remaining water while blending until desired texture is achieved.

Green Pineapple Smoothie

The pineapple and banana in this smoothie balance the bracingly bitter flavors of the greens.

INGREDIENTS | MAKES 3–4 CUPS

½ cup chopped dandelion greens
½ cup arugula
2 cups chopped pineapple
1 medium banana, peeled
2 cups coconut milk, divided

1. Place dandelion greens, arugula, pineapple, banana, and 1 cup coconut milk in a blender and blend until thoroughly combined.

2. Add remaining coconut milk while blending until desired texture is achieved.

Apple Peach Smoothie

Apples, peaches, and almond milk create a sweet, smooth blend that complements the green watercress. If you're looking for a healthy snack, skip the processed sweets and energy drinks and opt for this quick and easy blend that will give you sustainable energy for the rest of your day.

INGREDIENTS | MAKES 3–4 CUPS

1 cup chopped watercress
3 medium peaches, pitted
2 medium apples, cored and peeled
2 cups almond milk, divided

1. Place watercress, peaches, apples, and 1 cup almond milk in a blender and blend until thoroughly combined.

2. Add remaining almond milk while blending until desired texture is achieved.

Ginger Apple Smoothie

The fiber from the romaine and apples offers the benefit of an optimal digestive system, and the ginger soothes any stomach discomfort. This recipe is highly recommended for those days when you may feel irregular or uncomfortable.

INGREDIENTS | MAKES 3–4 CUPS

1 cup chopped romaine lettuce

3 medium apples, cored and peeled

1 tablespoon minced peeled gingerroot

2 cups almond milk, divided

1. Place romaine, apples, gingerroot, and 1 cup almond milk in a blender and blend until thoroughly combined.

2. Add remaining almond milk while blending until desired texture is achieved.

Fiber and Ginger Combination

Gingerroot is hailed as one of nature's most potent medicinal plants, with its most well-known cure being for stomach ailments. Combining ginger with the fiber found in fruits and leafy greens is an effective way to clean out the digestive tract, promote the release of good digestive enzymes, and soothe the stomach.

Cherry-Pear Smoothie

Try making this smoothie with frozen fruit and ice-cold almond milk for a delicious shake.

INGREDIENTS | MAKES 3–4 CUPS

1 cup chopped iceberg lettuce
2 medium pears, cored
1 medium banana, peeled
1 cup pitted cherries
½ teaspoon vanilla bean pulp
2 cups almond milk, divided

1. Place lettuce, pears, banana, cherries, vanilla bean pulp, and 1 cup almond milk in a blender and blend until thoroughly combined.

2. Add remaining almond milk while blending until desired texture is achieved.

Chocolate Banana Smoothie

Bursting with flavor, this smoothie provides vitamins, minerals, and antioxidants, even though it tastes like a creamy chocolate shake.

INGREDIENTS | MAKES 3–4 CUPS

1 cup chopped romaine lettuce
2 medium bananas, peeled
1 tablespoon cocoa powder
½ vanilla bean pulp
2 cups almond milk, divided

1. Place romaine, bananas, cocoa powder, vanilla bean pulp, and 1 cup almond milk in a blender and blend until thoroughly combined.

2. Add remaining almond milk while blending until desired texture is achieved.

Fight Cancer with Cocoa

With raw carob or cocoa powder, your kitchen can be turned into a chocolate shop of homemade delectable delights! Providing strong cancer-fighting antioxidants, these raw forms of chocolate bliss can extend your life while satisfying your sweet tooth.

Citrus Berry Smoothie

This refreshing smoothie is perfect for an after-workout snack. It's loaded with vitamins and antioxidants.

INGREDIENTS | MAKES 3–4 CUPS

1 cup chopped watercress
2 medium oranges, peeled
1 cup strawberries
1 cup blueberries
1 cup coconut milk, divided

1. Place watercress, oranges, strawberries, blueberries, and ½ cup coconut milk in a blender and blend until thoroughly combined.

2. Add remaining coconut milk while blending until desired texture is achieved.

Tart Pear Smoothie

Providing essential vitamins and minerals needed for the optimal functioning of your mind and body, this smoothie is a sweet, tart, and smart way to pep up your day.

INGREDIENTS | MAKES 4–6 CUPS

4 cups chopped romaine lettuce
4 medium pears, cored
1 medium banana, peeled
6 tablespoons lemon juice
2 cups water, divided

1. Place romaine, pears, banana, lemon juice, and 1 cup water in a blender and blend until thoroughly combined.

2. Add remaining water while blending until desired texture is achieved.

Guacamole Smoothie

This vibrant smoothie includes all of the wonderful ingredients
of the much-loved, extremely healthy snack.

INGREDIENTS | MAKES 3–4 CUPS

1 cup chopped watercress
1 medium avocado, pitted and peeled
1 medium lime, peeled
1 medium tomato
1 green onion, chopped
1 stalk celery
¼ cup cilantro
1 cup water, divided

1. Place watercress, avocado, lime, tomato, onion, celery, cilantro, and ½ cup water in a blender and blend until thoroughly combined.

2. Add remaining water while blending until desired texture is achieved.

Zucchini Apple Smoothie

Many people heavily season zucchini when preparing it as a side dish due to its somewhat bland taste. In this recipe, no seasonings are needed! The sweet carrots and apples blend beautifully with the spinach and zucchini to deliver maximum flavor.

INGREDIENTS | MAKES 3–4 CUPS

1 cup spinach

1 medium zucchini, chopped

3 medium carrots, peeled and chopped

2 medium apples, cored and peeled

2 cups water, divided

1. Place spinach, zucchini, carrots, apples, and 1 cup water in a blender and blend until thoroughly combined.

2. Add remaining water while blending until desired texture is achieved.

Benefits of Raw Zucchini

Raw-food enthusiasts embrace the idea of consuming minimally cooked foods because heat (above 115°F) reduces the vitamins, minerals, phytonutrients, and antioxidants found in fruits and vegetables. By blending raw zucchini into your smoothie, you'll benefit from it in its purest and healthiest form.

Sweet Asparagus Smoothie

Tangy citrus and healthy greens combine to create a tart and refreshing smoothie.

INGREDIENTS | MAKES 3–4 CUPS

1 cup chopped watercress
1 cup chopped asparagus
1 small lemon, peeled
1 large orange, peeled
1 cup water, divided

1. Place watercress, asparagus, lemon, orange, and ½ cup water in a blender and blend until thoroughly combined.

2. Add remaining water while blending until desired texture is achieved.

Orange Broccoli Smoothie

Thanks to the fiber, vitamins, and minerals in each of these ingredients, this smoothie is tasty and hearty enough to replace a meal.

INGREDIENTS | MAKES 3–4 CUPS

1 cup chopped romaine lettuce
1 cup chopped broccoli
1 medium zucchini, chopped
2 medium carrots, peeled and chopped
2 cups water, divided

1. Place romaine, broccoli, zucchini, carrots, and 1 cup water in a blender and blend until thoroughly combined.

2. Add remaining water while blending until desired texture is achieved.

Green Sweet Citrus Smoothie

This recipe is a wonderfully refreshing option for any time you may need a boost. The mildly peppery taste of watercress combines with the citrus flavors to develop a light and refreshing vitamin-packed treat.

INGREDIENTS | MAKES 3–4 CUPS

1 cup chopped watercress
1 large grapefruit, peeled
2 medium oranges, peeled
1 (½") piece gingerroot, peeled
½ lemon, peeled
1 cup water, divided

1. Place watercress, grapefruit, oranges, gingerroot, lemon, and ½ cup water in a blender and blend until thoroughly combined.

2. Add remaining water while blending until desired texture is achieved.

Farmers' Market Smoothie

If you're in the mood for a refreshingly savory smoothie, this one might be just what you're looking for! The ingredients create a splendid smoothie that may be delicious and filling enough to take the place of dinner.

INGREDIENTS | MAKES 4–6 CUPS

1 cup chopped romaine lettuce
2 medium tomatoes
1 medium zucchini, chopped
2 stalks celery, chopped
1 medium cucumber, chopped
½ cup chopped green onions
2 cloves garlic, peeled
2 cups water, divided

1. Place romaine, tomatoes, zucchini, celery, cucumber, green onions, garlic, and 1 cup water in a blender and blend until thoroughly combined.

2. Add remaining 1 cup water, if needed, while blending until desired texture is achieved.

CHAPTER 10

Side Dishes

Sautéed Celery and Almonds

Cooked celery is a vegetable that not many have tried, but it is very delicate and delicious. It is a good accompaniment to any favorite recipe. Celery leaves, which are not often used in recipes, are a good source of beta carotene and other antioxidants that help lower the risk of cancer. And celery is a good source of fiber, vitamin K, and folic acid.

INGREDIENTS | SERVES 6

2 tablespoons olive oil

2 cloves garlic, peeled and minced

3 cups sliced celery

¼ cup water

1 tablespoon coconut aminos

½ teaspoon five-spice powder

½ cup chopped celery leaves

⅛ teaspoon crushed red pepper flakes

⅓ cup sliced almonds, toasted

1. In large saucepan, heat olive oil over medium heat. Add garlic; cook for 1 minute.

2. Add celery; cook for 2–3 minutes or until crisp-tender. Add water and coconut aminos; bring to a simmer. Cover pan, reduce heat, and simmer for 4 minutes.

3. Uncover pan and add five-spice powder, celery leaves, and crushed red pepper flakes; cook for 2 minutes longer. Sprinkle with almonds and serve immediately.

Onions and Apples

This is an old-fashioned recipe that has fallen out of style, but it's delicious and easy to make. Choose tart apples that are firm but not too sweet, such as Granny Smith or Braeburn.

INGREDIENTS | SERVES 4

1 tablespoon coconut oil

1 tablespoon olive oil

2 medium onions, peeled and chopped

2 cloves garlic, peeled and minced

3 medium apples, peeled, cored, and sliced

3 tablespoons maple syrup

1 tablespoon lemon juice

½ teaspoon salt

½ teaspoon dried thyme leaves

1. In large pan, melt coconut oil and olive oil over medium heat. Add onions and garlic and cook until crisp-tender, about 4 minutes.

2. Add apples and stir. Drizzle with maple syrup and lemon juice and sprinkle with salt and thyme leaves.

3. Cover and cook on low for about 7–9 minutes or until apples are tender. Serve immediately.

Cajun Collard Greens

Like Brussels sprouts and kimchi, collard greens are one of those foods folks tend to either love or hate. They're highly nutritious, so hopefully this recipe will turn you into a collards lover, if you're not already.

INGREDIENTS | SERVES 4

2 tablespoons olive oil

1 medium onion, peeled and diced

3 cloves garlic, peeled and minced

1 pound collard greens, chopped

¾ cup water or Basic Vegetable Stock (see recipe in Chapter 6)

1 (14-ounce) can diced tomatoes, drained

1½ teaspoons Cajun seasoning

½ teaspoon hot sauce

¼ teaspoon salt

1. In a large skillet, heat olive oil over medium heat. Add onion, garlic, and collard greens and sauté for 3–5 minutes until onions are soft.

2. Add water or vegetable stock, tomatoes, and Cajun seasoning. Bring to a simmer over low heat, cover, and allow to cook for 20 minutes, or until greens are soft, stirring occasionally.

3. Remove lid, stir in hot sauce and salt, and cook, uncovered, for another 1–2 minutes, to allow excess moisture to evaporate.

How to Prepare Collards

Give your collards a good rinse, then tear the leaves off the middle stem. Fold or roll all the leaves together, then run a knife through them to create thin strips, similar to a chiffonade cut used for herbs. The stems can be added to a vegetable broth or your compost pile.

Green Bean Amandine

Fresh green beans are so much tastier than the frozen or canned variety! Try preparing them with almonds and mushrooms in this easy, rhyming Green Bean Amandine.

INGREDIENTS | SERVES 4

1 pound fresh green beans, trimmed and chopped

2 tablespoons olive oil

⅓ cup sliced almonds

¾ cup sliced mushrooms

½ medium yellow onion, peeled and chopped

½ teaspoon lemon juice

1. Fill a medium saucepan with cold salted water and bring to a boil over high heat. Add beans and cook until they are a vibrant green, about 3–4 minutes. Drain and rinse under cold water.

2. Heat olive oil in a large skillet over medium heat. Sauté almonds, mushrooms, and onion for 3–4 minutes, stirring frequently. Add green beans and lemon juice and heat for another 2 minutes.

Garlic and Gingered Green Beans

*Green beans are a staple in the Vegan Paleo diet. This recipe
jazzes them up with delicious garlic and ginger.*

INGREDIENTS | SERVES 4

1 pound fresh green beans, trimmed
and chopped

2 tablespoons olive oil

4 cloves garlic, peeled and minced

1 teaspoon minced fresh ginger

½ teaspoon crushed red pepper flakes

1 teaspoon salt

½ teaspoon ground black pepper

1. Fill a medium saucepan with cold salted water and
   bring to a boil over high heat. Add beans and cook
   until they are a vibrant green, about 3–4 minutes.
   Drain and rinse under cold water.

2. Heat olive oil in a large skillet. Add garlic, ginger, green
   beans, and red pepper flakes. Cook, stirring frequently,
   for 3–4 minutes until garlic is soft.

3. Season with salt and pepper.

Rosemary-Thyme Green Beans

In this recipe, the slow cooker acts like a steamer, resulting in tender green beans.

INGREDIENTS | SERVES 4

1 pound green beans
1 tablespoon minced rosemary
1 teaspoon minced thyme
2 tablespoons lemon juice
2 tablespoons water

1. Place all ingredients in a 2-quart slow cooker. Stir to distribute spices evenly.

2. Cook on low for 1½ hours or until green beans are tender. Stir before serving.

Lemon-Garlic Green Beans

Lemon zest and sliced garlic add a fresh and bright flavor to these slow-cooked green beans. Fresh green beans are sturdy enough to withstand very long cooking times without getting mushy.

INGREDIENTS | SERVES 4

1½ pounds fresh green beans, trimmed

3 tablespoons olive oil

3 large shallots, peeled and cut into thin wedges

6 cloves garlic, peeled and sliced

1 tablespoon grated lemon zest

½ teaspoon ground black pepper

½ cup water

1. Place green beans in a greased (with coconut oil) 4-quart slow cooker. Add remaining ingredients over the top of the beans.

2. Cook on high for 4–6 hours or on low for 8–10 hours. If you like your beans crisper, check them after about 3½ hours on high or after about 6 hours on low.

Mediterranean Green Beans

This simple recipe can be served hot or at room temperature. Add any leftovers to salads as a nice healthy addition.

INGREDIENTS | SERVES 4

1 pound fresh green beans, trimmed and cut into 1" pieces

2 teaspoons minced fresh rosemary

1 teaspoon grated lemon zest

1 tablespoon olive oil

½ teaspoon ground black pepper

1. Fill a medium saucepan with cold salted water and bring to a boil over high heat. Add beans and cook until they are a vibrant green, about 4 minutes.

2. Drain beans and transfer to a large bowl. Add remaining ingredients and toss to coat evenly. Serve warm or at room temperature.

Taking Care of Your Produce

It is best to store unwashed fresh green beans in a plastic bag in the refrigerator. When you are ready to use the beans, wash them under cold running water. Washing fruits and vegetables right before you use them keeps them fresher and prevents mold from spoiling the final product.

Broccoli and Bell Peppers

This colorful side dish is delicious and easy and very good for you. Broccoli is a cruciferous vegetable with cancer-fighting properties, and bell peppers are a great source of vitamin C and fiber. There are many colors of bell peppers on the market, from red to green to orange and even white and purple. Use what you like best.

INGREDIENTS | SERVES 4

1 head broccoli

2 tablespoons coconut oil

1 medium onion, peeled and chopped

1 medium red bell pepper, seeded and chopped

1 medium orange bell pepper, seeded and chopped

3 cloves garlic, peeled and sliced

3 tablespoons water or Basic Vegetable Stock (see recipe in Chapter 6)

½ teaspoon salt

⅛ teaspoon ground black pepper

1. Cut the florets off the broccoli stems. Peel stems and cut into 1" slices. In a medium saucepan, steam broccoli until crisp-tender, about 3–4 minutes. Drain and set aside.

2. In large skillet, melt coconut oil over medium heat. Add onion and cook for 3 minutes.

3. Add bell peppers and cook for another 3 minutes, stirring occasionally. Add broccoli, garlic, water or stock, salt, and pepper to skillet. Bring to a simmer, then cover and simmer for 3–4 minutes until everything is hot.

Broccoli and Hazelnuts

Bored with your everyday broccoli? Here's an easy-to-make version with a little zing!

INGREDIENTS | SERVES 8

2 pounds broccoli florets, washed and trimmed

12 cloves garlic, peeled

½ teaspoon ground black pepper

1 cup large raw hazelnuts

2 tablespoons olive oil

Juice from 2 medium lemons

1. Place broccoli in a 4-quart slow cooker and add garlic, pepper, hazelnuts, olive oil, and lemon juice and toss.

2. Cover and cook on high for 2 hours or on low for 4 hours.

Roasted Brussels Sprouts with Apples

Brussels sprouts are surprisingly delicious when prepared properly, so if you have bad memories of being force-fed soggy, limp baby cabbages as a child, don't let that stop you from trying this recipe!

INGREDIENTS | SERVES 4

2 cups quartered Brussels sprouts

8 cloves garlic, peeled

2 tablespoons olive oil

2 tablespoons apple cider vinegar

¾ teaspoon salt

½ teaspoon ground black pepper

2 medium apples, peeled, cored, and chopped

Reuse and Recycle!

Recycle this basic recipe by adding an extra garnish or two each time you make it: a touch of fresh rosemary, warm autumn spices, or chopped toasted nuts for crunch. For a Thanksgiving side dish, toss in some dried cranberries.

1. Preheat oven to 425°F.

2. Arrange Brussels sprouts and garlic in a single layer on a baking sheet. Drizzle with olive oil and apple cider vinegar and season with salt and pepper. Roast for 10–12 minutes, tossing once.

3. Remove tray from oven and add apples, tossing gently to combine. Roast for 10 more minutes or until apples are soft, tossing once again.

Cauliflower "Rice"

Cauliflower makes a surprisingly delicious substitute for rice. The creamy flesh of this cruciferous vegetable shreds nicely to mimic the texture of the grain. Just be sure you don't overcook it. You want each little piece of cauliflower to be tender, but slightly firm to stand up to the sauces and foods you'll serve with it.

INGREDIENTS | SERVES 4

1 head cauliflower

1 tablespoon lemon juice

2 tablespoons coconut oil

3 small shallots, peeled and minced

2 cloves garlic, peeled and minced

1 teaspoon salt

⅛ teaspoon ground white pepper

1. Rinse cauliflower and pat dry. Break into florets. Using a box grater or a food processer, grate or process the florets until they are in tiny pieces. Toss with lemon juice and set aside.

2. In a large skillet, melt coconut oil over medium-high heat. Add shallots and garlic; cook and stir until tender, about 5 minutes.

3. Add the cauliflower and sprinkle with salt and pepper. Cook for 4–5 minutes, stirring frequently, until cauliflower is tender but with some firmness in the center. Serve immediately.

Sweet and Savory Acorn Squash

This rich-tasting, sweet side serves well as a substitute for the starch often called for in recipes. This is so flavorful and filling, it can also suffice as a main lunchtime dish.

INGREDIENTS | SERVES 4

¾ cup maple syrup

1 teaspoon ground cinnamon

1 teaspoon ground nutmeg

2 small acorn squash, halved and seeded

¾ cup raisins

4 tablespoons coconut butter

½ cup water

1. In a small bowl, combine maple syrup, cinnamon, and nutmeg. Spoon maple syrup mixture into the squash halves. Sprinkle with raisins.

2. Top each half with 1 tablespoon coconut butter.

3. Wrap each squash half individually in aluminum foil and seal tightly. Pour water into a 4–6-quart slow cooker. Place wrapped squash, cut side up, in the slow cooker. Cover and cook on high for 4 hours or until squash is tender.

4. Open the foil packets carefully to allow steam to escape.

Butternut Squash with Walnuts and Vanilla

Butternut squash has a very mild and slightly sweet flavor. Many grocery stores now sell butternut squash that has been peeled and precut into cubes, which can make meal preparation a breeze.

INGREDIENTS | SERVES 4

1 (2-pound) butternut squash, peeled, seeded, and cut into 1" cubes

½ cup water

½ cup maple syrup

1 cup chopped walnuts

1 teaspoon cinnamon

4 tablespoons coconut butter

2 teaspoons grated fresh ginger

1 teaspoon vanilla

1. Grease a 4-quart slow cooker with olive oil. Add squash and water to slow cooker.

2. In a small bowl mix together maple syrup, walnuts, cinnamon, coconut butter, ginger, and vanilla. Drizzle maple syrup mixture evenly over butternut squash.

3. Cook on high for 4 hours or on low for 6–8 hours, or until squash is fork tender.

Cinnamon Toasted Butternut Squash

This side dish or snack is a great fall dish. It smells amazing and will give you the carbohydrate boost you need.

INGREDIENTS | SERVES 4

3 cups cubed butternut squash
1 tablespoon ground cinnamon
1 teaspoon nutmeg

1. Preheat oven to 350°F.

2. Place squash in 9" × 11" baking dish. Sprinkle with cinnamon and nutmeg.

3. Bake for 30 minutes or until tender and slightly brown.

Candied Butternut Squash

Use precut and peeled squash for an incredibly easy side dish.

INGREDIENTS | SERVES 4

4–5 cups cubed butternut squash

⅓ cup maple syrup

1 tablespoon orange zest

½ teaspoon ground cinnamon

½ teaspoon ground cloves

Add all ingredients to a greased (with coconut oil) 4-quart slow cooker. Cook on high for 3–4 hours or on low for 6–8 hours until squash is fork tender.

Butternut Squash Versus Sweet Potatoes

Wondering which might be better for you? Actually both are extremely healthy choices. Per serving, sweet potatoes have more fiber than the squash, but one cup of butternut squash contains fewer calories and fewer total carbohydrates. Both are high in vitamins A and C. In many recipes, they can be used interchangeably.

Maple-Glazed Roasted Vegetables

These easy roasted vegetables make an excellent holiday side dish. The vegetables can be roasted in advance and reheated with the glaze to save time if needed.

INGREDIENTS | SERVES 4

3 medium carrots, peeled and chopped

2 small parsnips, chopped

2 medium sweet potatoes, peeled and chopped

2 tablespoons olive oil

1 teaspoon salt

½ teaspoon ground black pepper

⅓ cup maple syrup

2 tablespoons Dijon mustard

1 tablespoon apple cider vinegar

½ teaspoon hot sauce

1. Preheat oven to 400°F.

2. On a large baking sheet, spread out carrots, parsnips, and sweet potatoes in a single layer.

3. Drizzle with olive oil and season with salt and pepper. Roast for 40 minutes, tossing once.

4. In a small bowl, whisk together maple syrup, Dijon mustard, apple cider vinegar, and hot sauce.

5. Transfer roasted vegetables to a large bowl and toss well with maple mixture.

Root Love

This tangy and sweet glaze will lend itself well to a variety of roasted vegetables and combinations. Try it with roasted Brussels sprouts, beets, butternut or acorn squash, or even with roasted turnips or daikon radish.

Sweet Beets

New research has shown an association between nitrates, such as those naturally occurring in beets, and increased performance in endurance sports. Serve this dish warm or cold. Beets are a great addition to salads as well.

INGREDIENTS | SERVES 6

1½ pounds beets
2 cups hot water
¼ cup peeled, finely chopped red onion
¼ cup maple syrup
2 cloves garlic, peeled and minced
¼ cup raisins
4 tablespoons chopped toasted walnuts
2–3 tablespoons lemon juice
1 tablespoon coconut oil
1 teaspoon ground black pepper

1. Combine beets and water in a 4–6-quart slow cooker. Cover and cook on high for about 2–2½ hours or until beets are tender.

2. Drain and peel beets and cut into ¾" cubes. Combine cubed beets and remaining ingredients, except pepper, in the slow cooker.

3. Cover and cook on high for 20–30 minutes. Season with pepper.

Maple-Roasted Carrots

Carrots are naturally sweet, and their sweetness intensifies when they are cooked.
They are especially good when paired with the sweetness of maple syrup.

INGREDIENTS | SERVES 6

1 tablespoon coconut oil

2 tablespoons maple syrup

1 teaspoon coconut aminos

1 pound carrots, peeled and chopped

1. Preheat oven to 400°F. In large ovenproof saucepan, combine coconut oil and maple syrup and heat on stovetop until melted. Add coconut aminos and carrots; cook and stir for 2 minutes.

2. Place the pan in the oven and roast for 15–20 minutes, turning once, or until carrots are tender and glazed. Serve immediately.

Glazed Carrots

The slow cooker is an excellent tool for preparing carrots. Just
be sure to allow enough time for them to cook.

INGREDIENTS | SERVES 3

3 cups thinly sliced carrots

2 cups water

¼ teaspoon lemon juice

3 tablespoons coconut butter

2 tablespoons chopped pecans

3 tablespoons maple syrup

1. Combine carrots, water, and lemon juice in 2-quart or smaller slow cooker. Cover and cook on high for 2–3 hours or until carrots are fork tender.

2. Drain well; return carrots to slow cooker and stir in remaining ingredients.

3. Cover and cook on high for 20–30 minutes.

Citrus-Steamed Carrots

If you've never tried figs with carrots, you're in for a treat!

INGREDIENTS | SERVES 6

1 cup orange juice

2 tablespoons lemon juice

2 tablespoons lime juice

1 pound carrots, peeled and julienned

3 medium fresh figs

1 tablespoon extra-virgin olive oil

1 tablespoon capers

1. In a saucepan over medium-high heat, combine orange juice, lemon juice, lime juice, and carrots. Cover and cook until carrots are tender, about 10 minutes. Remove from heat and cool.

2. Cut figs into wedges. Mound carrots on serving plates and arrange figs around carrots. Sprinkle olive oil and capers on top before serving.

Moroccan Root Vegetables

Root vegetables are flavored with Moroccan spices for a twist on an everyday favorite.

INGREDIENTS | SERVES 8

1 pound parsnips, peeled and diced
1 pound turnips, peeled and diced
2 medium onions, peeled and chopped
1 pound carrots, peeled and diced
6 dried apricots, chopped
4 pitted prunes, chopped
1 teaspoon ground turmeric
1 teaspoon ground cumin
½ teaspoon ground ginger
½ teaspoon ground cinnamon
¼ teaspoon ground cayenne pepper
1 tablespoon dried parsley
1 tablespoon dried cilantro
14 ounces Basic Vegetable Stock (see recipe in Chapter 6)

1. Add parsnips, turnips, onions, carrots, apricots, prunes, turmeric, cumin, ginger, cinnamon, cayenne pepper, parsley, and cilantro to a 4–6-quart slow cooker.

2. Pour in stock. Cover and cook on low for 9 hours or until vegetables are cooked through.

Turnip Tots

Here's a Paleo-approved substitute for a comfort-food favorite. Serve them with Homemade Ketchup (see recipe in Chapter 12).

INGREDIENTS | SERVES 4

4 medium turnips, peeled and cubed
2 tablespoons olive oil
2 tablespoons maple syrup
1 tablespoon brown mustard
¼ teaspoon ground black pepper

1. Place turnips in a 2- or 4-quart slow cooker, drizzle with olive oil and toss.

2. In a small bowl, mix together remaining ingredients. Drizzle over turnips and mix well.

3. Cover and cook on low for 5 hours.

Chipotle-Lime Mashed Sweet Potato

Sweet potatoes are a great post-workout food. These chipotle-lime mashed potatoes will be a favorite at any family table.

INGREDIENTS | SERVES 10

3 pounds sweet potatoes, peeled and cubed

1½ tablespoons coconut oil

1¼ teaspoons chipotle powder

Juice from ½ large lime

Alternatives to Sweet Potatoes

If you don't like sweet potatoes, you can easily substitute some lower-glycemic-load vegetables such as rutabagas, turnips, or beets. Additionally, cauliflower makes a great fake "mashed potato" substitute.

1. In a large saucepan fitted with a steamer insert, heat 1" water over medium-high heat. Place sweet potatoes in steamer and steam until soft, approximately 5–8 minutes. Transfer to a large bowl.

2. In a small saucepan, heat coconut oil and whisk in chipotle powder and lime juice. Pour mixture over sweet potatoes and mash with fork or potato masher.

Jicama "Rice"

You can make "rice" out of jicama just as you can out of cauliflower! Jicama are slightly sweeter and a bit more starchy tasting than cauliflower. The knobby white root is low in calories and high in fiber and antioxidants. It's also a good source of vitamins C and B, in addition to magnesium, copper, and iron. The recipe for Cauliflower "Rice" also appears in this chapter; try both to see which one you like best.

INGREDIENTS | SERVES 4

1 large jicama
1 tablespoon lemon juice
2 tablespoons coconut oil
2 shallots, minced
½ teaspoon salt
⅛ teaspoon ground white pepper

1. Peel jicama and grate on a box grater or in the food processor. Sprinkle with lemon juice and mix.

2. In large skillet, melt coconut oil over medium heat. Add shallots; cook and stir until tender, about 4 minutes.

3. Add grated jicama to the skillet; cook and stir until jicama releases some of its water and the water evaporates, about 5–6 minutes. Taste jicama to see if it's tender. If not, cook another 1–2 minutes. Then sprinkle with salt and pepper and serve.

Sautéed Cabbage

If you like, add some shredded apple to the cabbage for a lovely sweet and savory dish.

INGREDIENTS | SERVES 6

3 tablespoons coconut oil
1 medium onion, peeled and chopped
3 cloves garlic, peeled and minced
4 cups chopped green cabbage
3 cups chopped red cabbage
¼ cup water
1 tablespoon coconut aminos
1 teaspoon salt
⅛ teaspoon ground black pepper

1. In large skillet, heat coconut oil over medium heat. Add onion and garlic; cook and stir until crisp-tender, about 4 minutes.

2. Add cabbages to the skillet and cook and stir for 4 minutes.

3. Add water, coconut aminos, salt, and pepper and bring to a simmer. Cover and cook for 5–8 minutes longer until cabbage is tender.

Sweet and Sour Red Cabbage

Cabbage is often overlooked when it comes to weekly meals, which is unfortunate considering how nutritious it is. The tart apples and lime juice give the cabbage a tangy pickled flavor.

INGREDIENTS | SERVES 6

1 large head red cabbage, sliced

2 medium onions, peeled and chopped

6 small tart apples, peeled, cored, and quartered

1 cup hot water

1 cup apple juice

⅓ cup maple syrup

⅔ cup lime juice

½ teaspoon caraway seeds

3 tablespoons coconut butter, melted

3 tablespoons olive oil

1. Place cabbage, onions, and apples in a 4-quart slow cooker that has been greased with coconut oil.

2. In a medium bowl whisk together water, apple juice, maple syrup, lime juice, and caraway seeds. Pour over cabbage.

3. Drizzle coconut butter and olive oil over everything and cover slow cooker. Cook on high for 3–4 hours or on low for 6–8 hours. Stir well before serving.

Sautéed Kale and Broccoli Rabe

Kale is a magnificent cruciferous vegetable, as is broccoli rabe. They are both leafy green vegetables with fabulous nutritional profiles. Both vegetables are bitter, so cook them until tender to reduce that flavor profile. Adding sweet vegetables, such as onion, can help add another layer of flavor.

INGREDIENTS | SERVES 4–6

1 bunch broccoli rabe, trimmed and cut into 2" pieces

1 bunch kale, trimmed and cut into 4" pieces

2 tablespoons olive oil

1 medium onion, peeled and chopped

3 cloves garlic, peeled and minced

2 tablespoons lemon juice

1 teaspoon salt

⅛ teaspoon ground white pepper

1. In a medium saucepan, steam broccoli rabe and kale for about 3 minutes. Drain and set aside.

2. In large skillet, heat olive oil over medium heat. Add onion and garlic; cook and stir until tender, about 5 minutes.

3. Add steamed broccoli rabe and kale to skillet; cook and stir for 3 minutes. Add lemon juice, salt, and pepper and cook for another 2–3 minutes until tender. Serve immediately.

Sautéed Fennel with Orange

Fennel is crunchy and a bit sweet, and is most often associated with Italian cuisine.

INGREDIENTS | SERVES 4

3 small fennel bulbs, halved
1 (13-ounce) can chopped tomatoes
Rind and juice from 1 small orange
2 tablespoons maple syrup
½ teaspoon ground black pepper

1. Place fennel in a 4–6-quart slow cooker.

2. In a large mixing bowl, combine remaining ingredients. Pour mixture over fennel.

3. Cover and cook on high for 4–5 hours.

"Steamed" Artichokes

Choose artichokes that are all the same size so they will finish cooking at the same time.

INGREDIENTS | SERVES 4

4 large artichokes
1 cup water
1 large lemon, cut into eighths
2 tablespoons lemon juice
1 teaspoon dried oregano

1. Place artichokes stem side down in an oval 4-quart slow cooker. Pour water into the bottom of the slow cooker. Add lemon slices, lemon juice, and oregano.

2. Cook on low for 6 hours or until leaves are tender.

Greek-Style Asparagus

A slight Mediterranean touch produces a delicious aroma and wonderful flavor.

INGREDIENTS | SERVES 8

1 pound asparagus, trimmed

1 (28-ounce) can petite diced tomatoes, undrained

½ cup peeled, chopped onion

4 cloves garlic, peeled and minced

¾ teaspoon dried oregano

¾ teaspoon basil

1 teaspoon ground black pepper

1. Combine all ingredients except pepper in 2-quart or smaller slow cooker and cover.

2. Cook on high for about 4½ hours or until asparagus is tender. Season with pepper.

Roasted Asparagus with Mixed Summer Squashes and Peppers

Don't skip this warm-weather dish if you can't find the mini sweet peppers; simply substitute sliced red, yellow, or green bell peppers.

INGREDIENTS | SERVES 4

¼ cup olive oil

3 tablespoons apple cider vinegar

1 tablespoon minced garlic

1 pound asparagus, stem ends trimmed

1 pound mixed summer squashes, thinly sliced

1 pound mini sweet peppers, stemmed and sliced in half lengthwise

2 medium jalapeño peppers, seeded and chopped

1 teaspoon seasoning salt

1. Preheat oven to 400°F.

2. In a small bowl, mix olive oil, vinegar, and garlic together and set aside.

3. Place all vegetables in a large roasting pan and toss. Pour olive oil mixture over top, lifting and gently mixing the vegetables so they are all coated with oil. Sprinkle with seasoning salt.

4. Roast uncovered for about 45 minutes or until vegetables begin to darken; stir occasionally. Serve hot.

Asparagus and Cashew Nuts

This flavorful dish is loaded with fresh, Asian-inspired flavors.

INGREDIENTS | SERVES 2

2 tablespoons olive oil

2 tablespoons sesame oil

1 teaspoon minced fresh gingerroot

1 bunch asparagus, ends trimmed and cut into 2" pieces

1 teaspoon red pepper flakes

½ cup chopped cashews

1. Heat olive oil and sesame oil in a wok or large skillet over low to medium heat. Add ginger and stir-fry until slightly brown, about 5 minutes.

2. Add asparagus and red pepper flakes, and stir-fry for 3 minutes. Add cashews.

3. Cook, stirring frequently, for about 5 minutes or until asparagus is tender.

Sesame Oil

Sesame oil is great for stir-frying. It has a high heat capacity and a relatively low smoke value, so it cooks well under higher heat conditions. Additionally, sesame oil adds a nice Asian flavor to meals cooked with the oil.

Roasted Peppers

Sweet, smoky roasted peppers are so versatile. Use them in salads or as a side dish, or purée them into a silky sauce.

INGREDIENTS | SERVES 6

¼ cup olive oil
2 large green bell peppers
2 large yellow bell peppers
2 large red bell peppers
6 cloves garlic, peeled and minced
1 teaspoon ground black pepper

1. Preheat grill or broiler.

2. Pour olive oil into a large bowl. Dip peppers in olive oil, then place peppers on grill or a broiler pan. Reserve remaining oil.

3. Grill or broil peppers, turning frequently, until skin is blistered and beginning to blacken. Place peppers in a paper bag and fold over the top of the bag. Let peppers steam in the bag for 10 minutes. Remove peppers from bag and peel off the blistered skin.

4. Slice peppers and return them to the bowl with olive oil, along with garlic and black pepper.

5. Serve at room temperature or store in the refrigerator for up to 3 days.

Roasted Kale

This is a simple recipe that yields a crisp, irresistible snack. You can also slice up some collard greens or Swiss chard as a substitute for kale, or mix them all together for a tasty medley.

INGREDIENTS | SERVES 2

6 cups kale
1 tablespoon extra-virgin olive oil
1 teaspoon garlic powder

1. Preheat oven to 375°F.

2. Trim kale by removing the tough stems and tearing the leaves into pieces roughly 2" square.

3. Place leaves in a medium bowl and toss with olive oil and garlic powder and then lay kale on a large baking sheet.

4. Roast for 5 minutes; turn kale over and roast for another 7–10 minutes, until kale turns brown and becomes paper-thin and brittle.

5. Remove from oven and serve immediately or cool and store in an airtight container.

CHAPTER 11

Fruits

Cinnamon Stewed Plums

Serve as a breakfast fruit or as a dessert with a sorbet.

INGREDIENTS | SERVES 4

½ cup maple syrup
1 cup water
⅛ teaspoon salt
1 tablespoon fresh lemon juice
1 cinnamon stick
1 pound fresh ripe plums (about 8 small or 6 medium), pitted

1. Combine all ingredients in a 2–4-quart slow cooker and cook on low for about 6 hours, or until plums are tender.

2. Serve warm, chilled, or at room temperature.

Apples Supreme

Enjoy the treasures of apple-picking season with this melt-in-your-mouth dish, which is another that can be served as a breakfast fruit or warm dessert.

INGREDIENTS | SERVES 8

4 medium Granny Smith apples, peeled, cored, and sliced
4 medium Golden Delicious apples, peeled, cored, and sliced
¾ cup maple syrup
½ teaspoon ground cinnamon
½ teaspoon ground cloves
½ cup coconut butter

Place apples in a 4-quart slow cooker and toss with remaining ingredients. Cover and cook on low for 4–5 hours. Serve warm.

Blackberry Jam

*This easy low-sugar jam doesn't need to be canned;
it will keep for up to a month in the refrigerator.*

INGREDIENTS | MAKES 1 QUART

3 cups fresh blackberries
1.75 ounces no-sugar pectin
½ cup maple syrup
¾ cup water

1. Place all ingredients in a 2-quart slow cooker. Stir.

2. Cook uncovered on high for 5 hours. Using a fork or potato masher, smash berries a bit until they are the texture you prefer. Pour jam into an airtight container.

3. Refrigerate overnight before using.

Peach Marmalade

You can spread this on a fruit dish, or try it on Soft Breakfast Bread (see recipe in Chapter 2).

INGREDIENTS | MAKES 8 CUPS

2 pounds peaches, peeled, pitted, and chopped

½ cup chopped dried apricots

1 (20-ounce) can pineapple tidbits in unsweetened juice, undrained

2 medium oranges

1 small lemon

2 cups maple syrup

2 (3") cinnamon sticks

Innovative Peach Marmalade Uses

By keeping this marmalade the consistency of applesauce you have the added versatility of using it as a condiment to top grilled vegetables, mixing it with a chili sauce to create a sweet and savory dipping sauce, or using it to replace applesauce in many different recipes.

1. Add peaches to a food processor or blender along with apricots and pineapple (with juice).

2. Remove zest from oranges and lemon and add to the food processor or blender. Cut oranges and lemon into quarters and remove any seeds, then add to the food processor or blender. Pulse until entire fruit mixture is pulverized. Pour into a greased (with coconut oil) 4–6-quart slow cooker.

3. Add maple syrup to the slow cooker and stir to combine with the fruit mixture. Add cinnamon sticks. Cover and cook on low for 4 hours or until mixture reaches the consistency of applesauce, stirring occasionally. When finished cooking, remove cinnamon sticks.

4. Store in covered glass jars in the refrigerator for up to 3–4 weeks. The marmalade can also be frozen for up to 6 months, or you can process and seal it into sterilized jars for longer storage.

Apple Butter

Depending on when you start this recipe, it can take up to two days to complete, but it is great for giving an "autumn-like" feel to just about any side dish, entrée, dessert, or even a hot or iced beverage.

INGREDIENTS | MAKES 5 CUPS

6 medium apples, peeled, cored, and quartered

½ tablespoon vanilla extract

⅔ cup maple syrup

1 teaspoon ground cinnamon

¼ teaspoon ground cloves

1. Place apples and vanilla extract in a 4–6-quart slow cooker. Cover and cook on low for 8 hours.

2. Mash apples with a fork. Stir in maple syrup, cinnamon, and cloves.

3. Cover and cook on low for 6 hours. Allow to cool at room temperature or in refrigerator for 1–2 hours. Serve chilled or at room temperature.

Amish Apple Butter

Traditionally flavored with warm spices, this condiment is called a "butter" due to its thick consistency and soft texture. Since apple butter needs a long, unhurried cooking period to caramelize the fruit and deepen the flavors, the slow cooker is the most suitable modern cooking appliance in which to make it.

INGREDIENTS | MAKES 8 CUPS

10 cups (about 5 pounds) peeled, cored, and quartered Gala apples

1 cup maple syrup

3 tablespoons lemon juice

1½ teaspoons ground cinnamon

½ teaspoon ground cloves

½ teaspoon allspice

Old-Fashioned Apple Butter Making

Apple butter used to be made in large copper pots that simmered over a hot fire all day long. It was often done by a church group or by a large family who could share the responsibility of stirring the pot throughout the long day to keep the mixture from burning. Once finished, the apple butter would be canned and sold to raise money for a good cause or shared among all who helped make it.

1. Place apples in a 4-quart slow cooker greased with coconut oil.

2. Pour maple syrup and lemon juice over apples and add cinnamon, cloves, and allspice. Stir to coat apples.

3. Cover and cook on low for 14–16 hours until apple butter is a deep, dark brown and is richly flavored.

4. Ladle into clean, sterilized jars and store covered in refrigerator for up to 6 weeks. You can also process and can the apple butter if you prefer.

Strawberry Jelly

This jelly pairs perfectly with Almond Butter (see recipe in Chapter 8). Try making an "AB & J" with Paleo Sandwich Bread (see recipe in Chapter 3).

INGREDIENTS | SERVES 24

1½ quarts ripe strawberries, washed and hulled

3¾ cups maple syrup

¼ cup lemon juice

1. Place strawberries in a 4-quart slow cooker. Stir in maple syrup and lemon juice. Cover and cook on high for 2½ hours, stirring twice.

2. Uncover and continue cooking 2 hours longer or until preserves have thickened, stirring occasionally.

3. Ladle into hot, sterilized half-pint jelly jars, seal, and store in the refrigerator for up to 2 weeks.

Pear Butter

Enjoy pear season all year long! Drizzle this butter over some fresh fruit salad for a sweet addition to a traditional breakfast favorite.

INGREDIENTS | SERVES 8

8 large pears of any variety, peeled, cored, and sliced

2 cups water

¾ cup maple syrup

Juice from 1 lemon

1 whole star anise

¼ teaspoon ground ginger

¼ teaspoon nutmeg

1. Place all ingredients in a 6-quart slow cooker, cover, and cook on low for 10–12 hours.

2. Uncover and cook on low for an additional 10–12 hours until thick and most of the liquid has been absorbed.

3. Allow to cool and remove star anise before puréeing in blender. Store in airtight canning jars.

Apricot Butter

Apricot butter makes a tasty substitute for orange marmalade.

INGREDIENTS | SERVES 8

5 large ripe apricots, peeled and pitted

1½ cups maple syrup

2 teaspoons ground cinnamon

1 teaspoon ground cloves

1½ tablespoons lemon juice

1. Place apricots in a food processor or blender and purée until smooth. Pour puréed apricots into a 4–6-quart slow cooker and add maple syrup, spices, and lemon juice. Mix well.

2. Cover and cook on high for 8–10 hours. Remove cover halfway through cooking. Stir periodically.

3. Store in refrigerator, in an airtight canning jar, or freeze.

Blueberry Butter Bliss

This antioxidant-rich spread is a blueberry lover's dream.

INGREDIENTS | SERVES 7

4 cups fresh blueberries

¾ cup maple syrup

Zest of ½ lemon

1 teaspoon cinnamon

¼ teaspoon grated nutmeg

1. Place blueberries in a food processor or blender and purée until smooth. Pour puréed blueberries into a 4–6-quart slow cooker and cover. Cook on low for 5 hours.

2. Remove lid and add maple syrup, lemon zest, and spices, mixing well. Turn heat up to high, and cook for another hour, uncovered.

3. Pour into sterilized canning jars and cover tightly. Process canning jars in boiling water for 10 minutes. Store unopened jars in a cool, dark place.

Blackberry and Apple Preserves

These preserves showcase a not-so-traditional combination of two widely enjoyed, versatile fruits.

INGREDIENTS | SERVES 13

2 pounds cooking apples, peeled, cored, and chopped

3 cups maple syrup

1¾ cups blackberries

2 tablespoons lemon juice

1 lemon rind, grated

1. Place all ingredients in a 4–6-quart slow cooker, cover, and cook on high for 4–5 hours, stirring periodically.

2. Pour jam into warmed canning jars and allow to cool.

3. Cover and store in refrigerator for up to 2 months.

Fig Jam

This versatile spread is sure to liven up any Paleo breakfast, whether added to a fruit dish or spread on Soft Breakfast Bread (see recipe in Chapter 2) or Paleo Sandwich Bread (see recipe in Chapter 3). Not only is it delicious; it's also loaded with fiber and phytonutrients.

INGREDIENTS | SERVES 25

2 pounds fresh figs, cut into eighths

1 cup maple syrup

½ cup water

1 lemon, diced, including the rind, seeds removed

3 tablespoons finely diced crystallized ginger

1. Add all ingredients to a 2–3-quart slow cooker. Cover and cook on high for 4 hours.

2. Remove cover and cook for an additional 1–2 hours until mixture reaches a jam-like consistency.

3. While still hot, pour into clean, sterilized 4-ounce jars and store covered in refrigerator for up to 3 weeks.

Fig and Ginger Spread

Use this lightly spiced spread as a breakfast fruit spread or to liven up a basic dessert.

INGREDIENTS | SERVES 25

2 pounds fresh figs

2 tablespoons minced fresh ginger

2 tablespoons lime juice

½ cup water

¾ cup maple syrup

1. Place all ingredients in a 2-quart slow cooker. Stir. Cook on low for 2–3 hours. Remove lid and cook an additional 2–3 hours until mixture has thickened.

2. Pour into airtight containers and refrigerate for up to 6 weeks.

Apple and Pear Spread

Make the most of in-season apples and pears in this easy alternative to apple or pear butter.

INGREDIENTS | MAKES 3 QUARTS

4 medium Winesap apples, peeled, cored, and sliced

4 medium Bartlett pears, peeled, cored, and sliced

1 cup water or pear cider

½ cup maple syrup

¼ teaspoon ginger

¼ teaspoon cinnamon

¼ teaspoon nutmeg

¼ teaspoon allspice

1. Place all ingredients in a 4-quart slow cooker. Cook on low for 10–12 hours.

2. Uncover and cook on low for an additional 10–12 hours or until thick and most of the liquid has evaporated.

3. Allow to cool completely, then pour into a food processor and purée. Pour into clean glass jars. Refrigerate for up to 6 weeks.

Cinnamon-Spiced Apple Butter

If you're using a less tart apple, add the maple syrup ¼ cup at a time, until you reach desired sweetness. Serve over a dessert or breakfast dish.

INGREDIENTS | SERVES 6

8 large Granny Smith apples, peeled, cored, and quartered

½ cup unsweetened apple juice

¾ cup maple syrup

2 teaspoons ground cinnamon

½ teaspoon allspice

½ teaspoon ground cloves

1. Place apples and juice in a 2-quart slow cooker. Cover and cook on high for 4 hours.

2. Use an immersion blender to purée apples. Stir in maple syrup, cinnamon, all spice, and cloves.

3. Reduce the temperature of the slow cooker to low. Cook uncovered for 2 hours or until apple butter is thick and dark. Store in the refrigerator for several weeks or freeze until needed.

Blackberry Compote

Try this on cooked pineapple or apples.

INGREDIENTS | SERVES 6

2 cups blackberries

¼ cup maple syrup

¼ cup water

Place all ingredients in a 2-quart slow cooker. Cook on low for 3 hours, remove the lid, and cook on high for 4 hours.

Strawberry-Rhubarb Compote

Try this over fruit salad or another sweet treat.

INGREDIENTS | MAKES 1½ CUPS

1 pound strawberries, diced

½ pound rhubarb, diced

2 tablespoons lemon juice

1 tablespoon lemon zest

1. Place all ingredients in a 3½–4-quart slow cooker. Cook on low for 2 hours.

2. Lightly mash with a potato masher.

3. Cook on high, uncovered, for 1 additional hour.

Rhubarb Facts

The leaves of the rhubarb plant are toxic, but the stalks are perfectly edible. Despite being a tart vegetable, rhubarb is most often served in sweet dishes, where its tartness contrasts with a sweeter ingredient like strawberries.

Strawberry Apple Soup

Cold soups make wonderful desserts, especially on hot summer nights. Use beautiful organic berries and apple juice for the best flavor in this refreshing recipe. Garnish with sliced berries and a sprig of fresh mint and serve in large flat soup bowls with silver spoons.

INGREDIENTS | SERVES 4

2 cups water, divided
¼ cup maple syrup
1 cinnamon stick
1½ cups unsweetened apple juice
2 cups sliced strawberries
1 tablespoon lemon juice
1 tablespoon arrowroot powder
1 teaspoon vanilla
Pinch salt

1. In large saucepan, combine 1½ cups water, maple syrup, cinnamon stick, and apple juice and simmer for 10 minutes. Remove and discard cinnamon.

2. Pour 1 cup of this mixture into blender or food processor. Add strawberries and purée. Return to saucepan along with lemon juice.

3. Dissolve arrowroot powder in ½ cup water and add to pan. Simmer for 4–5 minutes or until thickened. Add vanilla and salt.

4. Cover and chill for 3–4 hours before serving.

Blueberry Soup

If you can find wild blueberries, use them for this recipe. They are smaller and more intensely flavored than cultivated blueberries.

INGREDIENTS | SERVES 4

3 cups fresh blueberries, divided

2 cups water, divided

½ cup freshly squeezed orange juice

2 tablespoons lemon juice

1 cinnamon stick

2 tablespoons maple syrup

¼ teaspoon salt

2 tablespoons quick-cooking tapioca, ground in food processor or blender

1 teaspoon vanilla

1. In large saucepan, combine 2½ cups blueberries, 1 cup water, orange juice, lemon juice, cinnamon stick, maple syrup, and salt. Bring to a simmer over medium heat.

2. Reduce heat to low and simmer for 10 minutes or until blueberries pop.

3. Purée soup in batches in blender or food processor and return to pan.

4. Dissolve tapioca in remaining 1 cup water and add to the soup. Simmer for another 5 minutes until thickened.

5. Cool soup for 30 minutes, then stir in vanilla. Cover and refrigerate until cold. Stir in remaining ½ cup blueberries before serving.

Curried Apple Soup

Apples contain no fat, sodium, or cholesterol and are a good source of fiber, so eat up!

INGREDIENTS | SERVES 6

3 tablespoons olive oil

1 medium leek, trimmed and chopped

2 cloves garlic, peeled and minced

4 medium apples, peeled, cored, and chopped

1–2 tablespoons curry powder

4 cups Basic Vegetable Stock (see recipe in Chapter 6)

2 tablespoons lemon juice

1 teaspoon salt

⅛ teaspoon ground white pepper

1 cup coconut milk

1. Heat oil in large saucepan over medium-high heat. Add leek and garlic; cook and stir for 3 minutes. Then add apples; cook and stir for 4 minutes longer.

2. Add curry powder; cook and stir for 2 minutes.

3. Add stock and lemon juice; simmer until apples and leek are very soft, about 20–25 minutes.

4. Purée using an immersion blender, keeping some of the vegetables and fruit whole if you'd like.

5. Season with salt and pepper. Stir in coconut milk and heat for 1–2 minutes until steaming. Serve immediately.

Cantaloupe-Peach Soup

*Best when melons and peaches are at their prime, this refreshing soup
is both light and delicate, an idea! summer dessert.*

INGREDIENTS | SERVES 4

2 cups cubed cantaloupe

2 cups cubed peaches

1½ cups guava nectar

2 tablespoons fresh lime juice

2 tablespoons coconut sugar

1 cup sliced strawberries

1. Combine cantaloupe, peaches, guava nectar, lime juice, and sugar in a blender or food processor and purée until smooth. Chill.

2. To serve, spoon soup into individual bowls and garnish with strawberry slices.

Raspberry Coulis

A coulis is a thick sauce made from puréed fruits or vegetables. In this recipe, the slow cooking eliminates the need for puréeing because the fruit cooks down enough that straining is unnecessary. It's delicious as both a breakfast fruit spread and a sweet dessert topping.

INGREDIENTS | SERVES 8

12 ounces fresh or frozen raspberries

1 teaspoon lemon juice

2 tablespoons maple syrup

Place all ingredients in a 2-quart slow cooker. Mash gently with a potato masher. Cook on low for 4 hours uncovered. Stir before serving.

Taste, Taste, Taste

When using fresh berries, it is important to taste them prior to sweetening. One batch of berries might be tart while the next might be very sweet. Reduce or eliminate maple syrup if using very ripe, sweet berries.

Summer Berry Sauce

Drizzle this sauce over desserts and breakfast foods.

INGREDIENTS | SERVES 20

1 cup raspberries
1 cup blackberries
1 cup golden raspberries
½ cup water
½ teaspoon maple syrup

Place all ingredients in a 2-quart slow cooker. Lightly mash berries with the back of a spoon. Cover and cook on low for 2 hours, then uncover and cook on high for 30 minutes.

Awesome Applesauce

Serve this applesauce warm or chilled. Or freeze it for an icy, sweet summer treat!

INGREDIENTS | SERVES 6

3 pounds Jonathan apples, peeled, cored, and coarsely chopped
½ cup water
½ cup maple syrup
½ teaspoon ground cinnamon

1. Combine all ingredients except cinnamon in a 6-quart slow cooker and cover.

2. Cook on high until apples are very soft, about 2–2½ hours. Sprinkle with cinnamon just before serving.

Baked Apples

You will feel as if you're eating apple pie when you eat these, and your house will smell like Thanksgiving whenever you make them.

INGREDIENTS | SERVES 6

6 large Pink Lady apples
1 cup unsweetened coconut flakes
½ teaspoon ground cinnamon

1. Preheat oven to 350°F.

2. Remove cores from apples, leaving ½" intact at the bottom. Place apples in a medium baking dish.

3. Fill cavities with coconut flakes and sprinkle with cinnamon.

4. Bake for 10–15 minutes. Apples are done when they are completely soft and brown on top.

Poached Figs

Use these poached figs in any recipe that calls for cooked figs, or eat them as is.

INGREDIENTS | SERVES 4

8 ounces fresh figs

1 cup water

1 vanilla bean, split

1 tablespoon maple syrup

1. Put all ingredients into a 2-quart slow cooker. Cook on low for 5 hours or until figs are cooked through and starting to split.

2. Remove figs from poaching liquid and serve.

Shopping for Figs

Look for figs that are plump and soft but not squishy. The skin should not be split or oozing. Store figs in the refrigerator or in a cool, dark cabinet until ready to use.

Grilled Pineapple

Pineapple has a lovely sweet-tart flavor, and grilling intensifies it. The addition of maple syrup will make this a really special treat at any barbecue or party.

INGREDIENTS | SERVES 6

1 large pineapple, cored, peeled, and cut into 1" rings
¼ cup maple syrup
2 tablespoons finely chopped macadamia nuts

1. Coat grill rack with nonstick cooking spray and preheat grill.

2. Grill pineapple over medium heat for 5 minutes. Turn pineapple over and grill 5 more minutes.

3. Remove pineapple from grill and place on a serving platter. Brush with maple syrup and sprinkle with macadamia nuts.

Roasted Fruit

Roasting fruit brings out its sweetness and tenderness. Stone fruits roast the best; they retain their shape and texture even after cooking. Serve warm from the oven, or cool the fruit, cover, and chill it in the fridge for a few hours before serving.

INGREDIENTS | SERVES 6

4 medium peaches, pitted and cut into quarters

4 medium nectarines, pitted and cut into quarters

6 large apricots, pitted and cut in half

1 tablespoon olive oil

2 tablespoons lemon juice

½ teaspoon salt

½ teaspoon dried thyme leaves

⅛ teaspoon ground white pepper

1½ cups red grapes

1. Preheat oven to 400°F. Place peaches, nectarines, and apricots, cut side up, in a roasting dish. Drizzle with olive oil and lemon juice. Sprinkle with salt, thyme, and pepper.

2. Roast, uncovered, for 15 minutes. Add grapes to the pan and stir gently. Roast for another 5–10 minutes or until fruit is tender.

Stewed Cinnamon Apples

The longer these luscious apples are cooked, the softer they become.

INGREDIENTS | SERVES 4

1 teaspoon maple syrup
1 tablespoon ground cinnamon
2 tablespoons lemon juice
2 tablespoons water
4 medium apples, peeled, cored, and cut into wedges

1. Place maple syrup, cinnamon, lemon juice, and water in a 4-quart slow cooker. Stir until maple syrup dissolves. Add apples.

2. Cook on low for up to 8 hours. Stir before serving.

Pear Slush

This unusual summer treat will keep you hydrated on a hot day.

INGREDIENTS | SERVES 6

1 pound Bosc pears, peeled and cored
1¼ cups water
¼ cup maple syrup
½ teaspoon ground cinnamon
1 tablespoon lemon juice

Ice Fruit

Enjoy this deliciously cool, thirst-quenching treat as a postgame snack to cool down or as a pregame energizer for a last-minute burst of high-quality carbohydrates and fluids.

1. Place pears, water, maple syrup, and cinnamon in a 2-quart slow cooker. Cover and cook on high for 2½–3½ hours. Stir in lemon juice.

2. Process pear and syrup mixture in a blender until smooth. Strain mixture through a sieve, and discard any pulp.

3. Pour liquid into an 11" × 9" baking dish, cover tightly with plastic wrap, and transfer to freezer.

4. Stir every hour with a fork, crushing any lumps as it freezes. Freeze 3–4 hours or until firm.

Apple Freeze

If you like applesauce, you'll love Apple Freeze.

INGREDIENTS | SERVES 6

1 pound Golden Delicious apples, peeled, cored, and chopped

1¼ cups water

¼ cup maple syrup

½ teaspoon ground cinnamon

1 tablespoon lemon juice

1. Place apples, water, maple syrup, and cinnamon in a 2-quart slow cooker. Cover and cook on high for 2½–3½ hours. Stir in lemon juice.

2. Process apple and syrup mixture in a blender until smooth. Strain mixture through a sieve, and discard any pulp.

3. Pour liquid into an 11" × 9" baking dish, cover tightly with plastic wrap, and transfer to freezer.

4. Stir every hour with a fork, crushing any lumps as it freezes. Freeze 3–4 hours or until firm.

CHAPTER 12

Sauces and Spreads

Kale Pesto

Kale's cholesterol-reducing properties are stronger if it's cooked. Steaming reduces the leafy green's strong taste and helps it retain its bright color. It freezes well; freeze in small portions and thaw in the refrigerator overnight before using.

INGREDIENTS | MAKES 2½ CUPS

2 cups packed chopped fresh kale

1 cup fresh basil leaves

½ cup toasted chopped hazelnuts

1 tablespoon lemon juice

1 clove garlic, peeled and minced

½ teaspoon salt

⅛ teaspoon ground black pepper ·

⅓ cup olive oil

2 tablespoons hazelnut oil

¼ cup water

1. Bring 2 cups water to a boil in a medium saucepan. Place kale in a steamer basket or insert and put it in the pan. Cover. Steam kale for 2–3 minutes or until slightly softened. Remove to colander to drain. Press in kitchen towel to remove excess water.

2. Combine kale, basil, hazelnuts, lemon juice, garlic, salt, and pepper in a food processor. Process until finely chopped.

3. With motor running, add olive oil and hazelnut oil gradually through the feed tube. Add water as needed for desired consistency. Correct seasoning. Store, covered, in the refrigerator for up to a week or freeze for longer storage.

Spinach Pistachio Pesto

Pistachios add a lot of flavor to pesto without any dairy at all. It can be frozen in small amounts; just thaw in the fridge overnight before using in recipes.

INGREDIENTS | MAKES 3 CUPS

1 (10-ounce) package frozen chopped spinach

1½ cups shelled pistachios

1 cup fresh basil leaves

⅔ cup olive oil

1 teaspoon salt

¼ cup water

1. In blender or food processor, combine spinach, pistachios, and basil and blend until finely chopped.

2. With motor running, slowly add olive oil through the feed tube until mixture is smooth and thick. Add salt.

3. Add enough water for desired consistency. Refrigerate, covered, for up to 3 days, or freeze for longer storage.

Mint Pesto

Pesto can be made with just about any herb or vegetable. The sharp, sweet smell of mint is refreshing and an appetite stimulant. Mint is also rich in carotenes, which are precursors to vitamin A, and vitamin C.

INGREDIENTS | MAKES 2 CUPS

2 cups packed fresh mint leaves
1 clove garlic, peeled
2 tablespoons lemon juice
1/3 cup toasted pine nuts
1/4 teaspoon salt
1/3 cup extra-virgin olive oil
2–3 tablespoons water

1. In blender or food processor, chop mint with garlic until finely chopped.

2. Add lemon juice, pine nuts, and salt and process again until finely chopped.

3. With the machine running, add oil and water until a sauce forms. You may need to add more oil or water for desired consistency. Store covered in the refrigerator for up to 3 days; freeze for longer storage.

Chimichurri Sauce

Chimichurri comes from Argentina. This flavorful herb sauce is very easy to make. Store it covered in the refrigerator for up to five days. You can freeze it for longer storage; just thaw in the fridge overnight.

INGREDIENTS | MAKES 2 CUPS

1½ cups packed flat-leaf parsley

⅓ cup fresh cilantro or oregano leaves

1 medium shallot, peeled and chopped

3 cloves garlic, peeled and chopped

¼ cup apple cider vinegar

2 tablespoons lemon juice

⅔ cup olive oil

½ teaspoon salt

⅛ teaspoon ground black pepper

1. Combine parsley, cilantro, shallot, and garlic in food processor and process until finely chopped. You can chop all these ingredients by hand if you'd like.

2. Transfer to a medium bowl and add vinegar, lemon juice, olive oil, salt, and pepper; stir with a whisk until combined. Refrigerate until serving time.

Roasted Vegetable Salsa

Most salsas are made from raw vegetables. Roasting the vegetables adds
another layer of flavor and makes this salsa a bit different. Tomatillos look
like little green tomatoes, but they have a tart and fresh taste.

INGREDIENTS | MAKES 4 CUPS

½ pound fresh tomatillos, husked and coarsely chopped

½ pound Roma tomatoes, coarsely chopped

1 medium zucchini, coarsely chopped

2 tablespoons olive oil

1 medium onion, peeled and chopped

2 small jalapeño peppers, seeded and chopped

4 cloves garlic, peeled and chopped

2 tablespoons lemon juice

½ teaspoon salt

⅛ teaspoon ground black pepper

½ teaspoon crushed red pepper flakes

2 tablespoons chopped fresh cilantro

1. Preheat oven to 400°F. Place tomatillos, tomatoes, and zucchini on a rimmed baking sheet. Drizzle with olive oil and stir to coat. Top with onion.

2. Roast for 20–25 minutes or until vegetables are soft and light brown on the edges. Remove from oven and place in large bowl.

3. Stir in jalapeño peppers, garlic, lemon juice, salt, black pepper, red pepper flakes, and cilantro. Cool, then store in refrigerator.

Cashew Alfredo Sauce

Most vegan Alfredo recipes start with a roux of margarine and soy milk, but this one uses cashew cream instead for a sensually decadent white sauce. Serve this sauce over Slow-Cooked Spaghetti Squash (see recipe in Chapter 7), zucchini noodles, or roasted eggplant.

INGREDIENTS | SERVES 6

½ cup raw cashews
1¼ cups water
2 tablespoons lemon juice
2 tablespoons tahini
¼ cup peeled, diced onion
1 teaspoon minced garlic
½ teaspoon salt
¼ cup nutritional yeast
2 tablespoons olive oil

1. In a blender, process cashews and water until completely smooth and creamy, about 90 seconds.

2. Add remaining ingredients except oil and purée until smooth. Slowly add oil until mixture is thick and oil is completely blended in.

3. Heat in a saucepan over low heat for 4–5 minutes, stirring frequently.

Cucumber Raita

Raita is an Indian side dish that serves as a cooling complement to spicy dishes. It's usually made of cucumber, sour cream, and some herbs. Coconut milk is a vegan and Paleo alternative. Because cucumbers contain a lot of water, they are salted and left to drain before they are mixed with the coconut milk.

INGREDIENTS | SERVES 4–6

1 (5-ounce) can full-fat coconut milk
1 medium cucumber, peeled and seeded
½ teaspoon salt
⅓ cup minced red onion
1 clove garlic, peeled and minced
2 tablespoons lemon juice
1 tablespoon chopped fresh mint
½ teaspoon ground cumin
⅛ teaspoon ground white pepper

1. Refrigerate the can of coconut milk for at least 8 hours. Spoon off the solids from the top; reserve the thin liquid for another use.

2. Slice cucumber thinly and sprinkle with salt. Place in colander and place in the sink; let stand for 30 minutes. Rinse cucumber, drain, and pat dry with paper towels.

3. In medium bowl, combine coconut milk solids, cucumber, red onion, garlic, and lemon juice and mix well. Stir in mint, cumin, and pepper. Cover and chill for 1 hour before serving.

Eggplant Relish

Serve with grilled or raw veggies for dipping.

INGREDIENTS | SERVES 6

1 large eggplant, pierced all over with fork

2 tablespoons extra-virgin olive oil

½ cup finely chopped tomato

¼ cup peeled, finely chopped onion

¼ cup almond yogurt

3 cloves garlic, peeled and minced

½ teaspoon dried oregano leaves

1–2 tablespoons lemon juice

1 teaspoon ground black pepper

1. Place eggplant in a 4-quart slow cooker, cover, and cook on low until tender, 4–5 hours. Cool to room temperature.

2. Cut eggplant in half lengthwise and remove eggplant pulp (including seeds) from peel with a spoon. Mash eggplant pulp and mix with olive oil, tomato, onion, almond yogurt, garlic, and oregano. Season with lemon juice and pepper before serving.

Jalapeño-Tomatillo Sauce

This sauce is great for adding a little kick to your favorite dishes.

INGREDIENTS | SERVES 4

1 teaspoon olive oil
2 cloves garlic, peeled and minced
1 medium onion, peeled and sliced
7 large tomatillos, husked and diced
2 small jalapeño peppers, seeded and minced
½ cup water

1. Heat oil in a nonstick skillet over medium heat. Sauté garlic, onion, tomatillos, and jalapeño peppers for 5–10 minutes, until softened.

2. Place mixture in a 4-quart slow cooker. Add water and stir. Cook on low for 8 hours.

Fruity Balsamic Barbecue Sauce

Use this sauce on grilled vegetables or as a dipping sauce.

INGREDIENTS | SERVES 20

¼ cup apple cider vinegar
2½ cups cubed mango
2 chipotle peppers in adobo, puréed
1 teaspoon maple syrup

1. Place all ingredients in a 2-quart slow cooker. Stir. Cook on low for 6–8 hours.

2. Mash sauce with a potato masher. Store in an airtight container for up to 2 weeks in the refrigerator.

Artichoke Sauce

Slow cooking artichoke hearts gives them a velvety texture.

INGREDIENTS | SERVES 4

1 teaspoon olive oil

8 ounces frozen artichoke hearts, defrosted

3 cloves garlic, peeled and minced

1 medium onion, peeled and minced

2 tablespoons capers

1 (28-ounce) can crushed tomatoes

1. Heat oil in a nonstick skillet over medium heat. Sauté artichoke hearts, garlic, and onion for about 10–15 minutes until onions are translucent and most of the liquid has evaporated.

2. Put mixture into a 4-quart slow cooker. Stir in capers and crushed tomatoes.

3. Cook on high for 4 hours or on low for 8 hours.

Cleaning Slow Cookers

Do not use very abrasive tools or cleansers on a slow cooker insert. They may scratch the surface, allowing bacteria and food to leach in. Use a soft sponge and baking soda for stubborn stains.

Pink Tomato Sauce

Try this creamier version of classic spaghetti sauce over Slow-Cooked Spaghetti Squash (see recipe in Chapter 7); zucchini noodles, or a medley of oven-roasted vegetables.

INGREDIENTS | SERVES 8

1 tablespoon olive oil
1 large onion, peeled and diced
2 cloves garlic, peeled and minced
1 tablespoon minced fresh basil
1 tablespoon minced fresh Italian parsley
⅔ cup coconut or almond milk
1 stalk celery, diced
1 (14.5-ounce) can whole tomatoes in purée
1 (28-ounce) can crushed tomatoes

1. Heat olive oil in a medium nonstick skillet over medium heat. Sauté onion and garlic for 7–10 minutes until soft.

2. Add onion and garlic to a 6-quart slow cooker. Add herbs, milk, celery, and tomatoes. Stir to distribute spices. Cook on low for 10–12 hours.

Celery, the Star

Celery is often overlooked as an ingredient. It is perfect for slow cooking because it has a high moisture content but still remains crisp through the cooking process. Celery is also very low in calories and high in fiber.

Chipotle Tomato Sauce

Try this southwestern take on the classic Italian tomato sauce on Slow-Cooked Spaghetti Squash (see recipe in Chapter 7) or as a salsa with a southwestern dish.

INGREDIENTS | SERVES 6

3 cloves garlic, peeled and minced

1 large onion, peeled and minced

1 (28-ounce) can crushed tomatoes

1 (14.5-ounce) can diced tomatoes

3 chipotle peppers in adobo, minced

1 teaspoon dried oregano

1 tablespoon minced fresh cilantro

½ teaspoon ground black pepper

Place all ingredients in a 4-quart slow cooker. Cook on low for 8–10 hours. Stir before serving.

Know Your Slow Cooker

When using a new or new-to-you slow cooker for the first time, pick a day when someone can be there to keep tabs on it. In general, older slow cookers cook at a higher temperature than new models, but even new slow cookers can have some differences. It is a good idea to know the quirks of a particular slow cooker so food is not overcooked or undercooked. Tweak cooking times accordingly.

Spinach Marinara Sauce

Powerfully flavored and nutrient-rich, this sauce is delicious over a vegetable medley side dish or main course.

INGREDIENTS | SERVES 8

1 (28-ounce) can crushed tomatoes, with liquid

1 (10-ounce) package frozen chopped spinach, thawed and drained

2⅔ (6-ounce) cans tomato paste

1 (4.5-ounce) can sliced mushrooms, drained

1 medium onion, peeled and chopped

5 cloves garlic, peeled and minced

2 bay leaves

⅓ cup grated carrot

¼ cup olive oil

2½ tablespoons crushed red pepper

2 tablespoons lemon juice

2 tablespoons dried oregano

2 tablespoons dried basil

1. In a 4–6-quart slow cooker, combine all ingredients, cover, and cook on high for 4 hours.

2. Stir, reduce heat to low, and cook for 1–2 more hours.

Cranberry Sauce

Serve this sweet-tart cranberry sauce with a holiday meal, use it as a spread, or pour it over your favorite dessert.

INGREDIENTS | SERVES 10

12 ounces fresh cranberries
½ cup freshly squeezed orange juice
½ cup water
½ teaspoon orange zest
½ teaspoon maple syrup

Place all ingredients in a 1½–2-quart slow cooker. Cook on high for 2½ hours. Stir before serving.

Cran-Apple Sauce

This sauce is simple, sweet, and loaded with antioxidants including vitamin C.

INGREDIENTS | SERVES 6

1 cup fresh cranberries
8 medium apples, peeled, cored, and chopped
½ cup maple syrup
1 cinnamon stick, halved
6 whole cloves

1. Combine cranberries, apples, and maple syrup in a 4–6-quart slow cooker.

2. Place cinnamon and cloves in center of a 6" square of cheesecloth. Pull up around sides; tie to form pouch. Place in slow cooker.

3. Cover and cook on low for 4–5 hours or until cranberries and apples are very soft. Remove cheesecloth pouch and discard. Serve sauce warm or at room temperature.

Mango Chutney

This fruity, cool chutney is a nice accompaniment to spicy dishes. To peel a ripe mango, slide a spoon, bottom side up, under the skin to remove it easily without damaging the fruit.

INGREDIENTS | SERVES 8

3 medium mangoes, peeled and diced

1 small red onion, peeled and diced

½ cup chopped fresh cilantro

1 teaspoon lime juice

½ teaspoon lime zest

½ teaspoon ground black pepper

Combine all ingredients in a medium bowl and stir gently to combine. Serve at room temperature or refrigerate for 4 hours before serving.

Apple Chutney

Try this as a side dish for hearty winter squash dishes.

INGREDIENTS | SERVES 4

2 cups ice water

1 tablespoon lemon juice

3 large Granny Smith apples, cored and diced

1 medium shallot, peeled and thinly sliced

3 sprigs fresh mint, chopped

1 tablespoon lemon zest

¼ cup golden raisins

½ teaspoon ground cinnamon

1. Combine water and lemon juice in a large mixing bowl. Add apples and soak for 5 minutes.

2. Drain apples and mix them with remaining ingredients in a medium bowl.

Homemade Ketchup

Condiments like ketchup are generally gluten-free, but you always have to read the label and check with the manufacturer to make sure. Instead of worrying about unwanted ingredients, you can make your own and know exactly what is in your specially made ketchup!

INGREDIENTS | SERVES 5

1 (15-ounce) can no-salt-added tomato sauce

2 teaspoons water

½ teaspoon onion powder

¾ cup maple syrup

⅓ cup lime juice

¼ teaspoon ground cinnamon

⅛ teaspoon ground cloves

⅛ teaspoon ground allspice

⅛ teaspoon nutmeg

⅛ teaspoon freshly ground black pepper

⅔ teaspoon sweet paprika

1. Add all ingredients to a 2½-quart slow cooker. Cover and cook on low for 2–4 hours or until ketchup reaches desired consistency, stirring occasionally.

2. Turn off the slow cooker or remove the insert from the slow cooker. Allow mixture to cool, then put in a covered container (such as a recycled ketchup bottle). Store in the refrigerator for up to a month.

Ketchup with a Kick

If you like zesty ketchup, you can add crushed red peppers or salt-free chili powder along with, or instead of, the cinnamon and other seasonings. Another alternative is to use hot paprika rather than sweet paprika.

Red Pepper Relish

This sauce adds a little kick, spicing up the flavor of just about any entrée or side.

INGREDIENTS | SERVES 8

4 large red bell peppers, seeded and cut into thin strips

2 small sweet onions, peeled and thinly sliced

6 tablespoons lemon juice

¼ cup maple syrup

½ teaspoon dried thyme

½ teaspoon red pepper flakes

½ teaspoon ground black pepper

Combine all ingredients in a 1½-quart slow cooker and mix well. Cover and cook on low for 4 hours.

Caveman Caponata

This is an extremely flavorful, high-fiber, nutrient-dense vegetable entrée. The high fiber content makes this dish very filling.

INGREDIENTS | SERVES 4

1 pound plum tomatoes, chopped

1 eggplant, cut into ½" pieces

2 medium zucchini, cut into ½" pieces

3 stalks celery, sliced

1 large onion, peeled and finely chopped

½ cup chopped fresh parsley

1 teaspoon lemon juice

2 tablespoons lime juice

1 tablespoon maple syrup

¼ cup raisins

¼ cup tomato paste

¼ teaspoon freshly ground black pepper

Combine all ingredients in 4-quart slow cooker. Cover and cook on low for 5½ hours. Do not remove cover during cooking.

Pumpkin Butter

Smear this spiced spread on apple or pear slices, drizzle it over butternut squash, or warm it slightly and pour it on top of your favorite dessert.

INGREDIENTS | SERVES 8

6 cups pumpkin purée
2¼ cups maple syrup
1 teaspoon cinnamon
¾ teaspoon ground ginger
½ teaspoon ground cloves
¼ teaspoon ground nutmeg
Juice of 3 medium lemons

1. Add all ingredients to a 4–6-quart slow cooker. Cook mixture on low for about 4–4½ hours, until it becomes thick and smooth.

2. Pour finished pumpkin butter into sterilized pint or half-pint jars, and seal. Store in refrigerator.

Serrano-Mint Sauce

Try this spicy mint sauce over roasted cauliflower. It can also be used in place of other condiments or as a salad dressing.

INGREDIENTS | SERVES 6

1 cup tightly packed mint leaves

2 medium serrano chilies, seeded and chopped

4 cloves garlic, peeled

1 (1") piece fresh gingerroot, peeled and chopped

¼ cup lime juice

2 tablespoons olive oil

Combine all ingredients in food processor and pulse to coarsely blend.

Habanero-Basil Sauce

This sauce is very spicy and goes well with grilled eggplant or portobello mushrooms.

INGREDIENTS | SERVES 6

2 cups chopped fresh basil leaves

3 medium habanero peppers, seeded and chopped

2 cloves garlic, chopped

¼ cup lime juice

3 tablespoons olive oil

Combine all ingredients in food processor and pulse to coarsely blend.

Avocado-Eggplant Spread

Eggplant and avocado together make a filling and healthy dip. Add this recipe to salads or use as dip with cut vegetables.

INGREDIENTS | SERVES 4

2 medium eggplants, peeled and roughly chopped

2 tablespoons olive oil

¼ cup tahini

2 cloves garlic, peeled and chopped

2 tablespoons lime juice

½ teaspoon ground black pepper

½ teaspoon cumin

1 large avocado, pitted, peeled, and cubed

1. Preheat oven to 425°F.

2. In a large bowl, toss eggplant with olive oil. Place eggplant in a large roasting pan. Roast, stirring occasionally, until eggplant is soft, about 15–20 minutes.

3. Remove eggplant from roasting pan and place in the bowl of a food processor. Add remaining ingredients and pulse until slightly chunky.

"Butterscotch-Caramel" Sauce

Here is a sweet and delicious way to enhance the flavor of just about any dessert.

INGREDIENTS | SERVES 24

½ cup coconut butter

2 cups full-fat coconut milk

3 cups maple syrup

2 tablespoons fresh lemon juice

1 tablespoon vanilla extract

1. Add coconut butter, coconut milk, maple syrup, and lemon juice to a 2-quart or smaller slow cooker. Cover and cook on high for 1 hour or until coconut butter is melted and milk begins to bubble around the edges of the cooker. Uncover and stir.

2. Cover and cook on low for 2 hours, stirring occasionally.

3. Uncover and cook on low for 1 more hour or until the mixture coats the back of a spoon or the sauce reaches its desired thickness. Stir in vanilla.

CHAPTER 13

Nuts and Trail Mixes

Slow-Cooked Almonds with a Kick

Tl ese crunchy, heart-healthy snacks are hard to resist.

INGREDIENTS | SERVES 24

6 cups whole raw almonds

4 tablespoons coconut oil

3 cloves garlic, peeled and minced

2 teaspoons coarsely ground
black pepper

1. Heat a 4-quart slow cooker on high for 15 minutes. Add almonds. Drizzle oil over almonds and stir. Sprinkle with garlic and pepper and stir. Cover and cook on low for 2 hours, stirring every 30 minutes.

2. Turn heat up to high and cook uncovered for 30 minutes, stirring after 15 minutes.

3. Turn heat to low and serve warm or remove from heat and allow to cool.

Spiced Cashews

This fiery favorite can liven up any appetizer menu.

INGREDIENTS | SERVES 24

6 cups cashews

3 tablespoons olive oil

3 tablespoons crushed dried rosemary leaves

1 tablespoon maple syrup

¾ teaspoon cayenne pepper

½ teaspoon garlic powder

1. Heat a 2–4-quart slow cooker on high for 15 minutes; add cashews. Drizzle oil over cashews and toss to coat. Add remaining ingredients and stir to combine.

2. Cover and cook on low for 2 hours, stirring every hour. Turn heat to high, uncover, and cook for 30 minutes, stirring after 15 minutes.

3. Turn heat to low to keep warm for serving or remove from slow cooker.

Hot Cinnamon-Chili Walnuts

These seasoned walnuts are a surprising hit with the combined punch of chili powder and cinnamon.

INGREDIENTS | SERVES 6

1½ cups walnuts
¼ cup maple syrup
2 teaspoons cinnamon
1½ teaspoons chili powder
2 teaspoons coconut oil

1. Combine all ingredients in a greased (with olive oil) 2½-quart slow cooker.

2. Cover slow cooker and vent lid with a chopstick or the handle of a wooden spoon. Cook on high for 2 hours or on low for 4 hours. If using a larger slow cooker, you will probably need to reduce the cooking time to only 1 hour on high or 2 hours on low.

3. Line a baking sheet with parchment paper. Pour walnut mixture onto the baking sheet and spread out into one layer. Allow to cool and dry and then transfer to a container with an airtight lid. Store in the pantry for up to 2 weeks.

Roasted Pistachios

Raw pistachios are available at Trader Joe's and health food stores. Roasting your own lets you avoid salt on the nuts, which makes them a snack that perfectly matches your healthy palate.

INGREDIENTS | SERVES 16

1 pound raw pistachios
2 tablespoons extra-virgin olive oil

Putting Roasted Pistachios to Work

You can make 8 servings of a delicious coleslaw alternative by mixing together 3 very thinly sliced heads of fennel; ½ cup roasted, chopped pistachios; 3 table-spoons extra-virgin olive oil; 2 tablespoons freshly squeezed lemon juice; and 1 tea-spoon finely grated lemon zest. Add freshly ground black pepper and additional lemon juice if desired. Serve immediately or cover and refrigerate for up to 1 day.

1. Add nuts and oil to a 2-quart slow cooker. Stir to combine. Cover and cook on low for 1 hour.

2. Stir mixture again. Cover and cook for 2 more hours, stirring mixture again after 1 hour. Cool and store in an airtight container.

Spiced Walnuts

Here's a perfect sweet and savory snack, guaranteed to please snackers and party guests.

INGREDIENTS | SERVES 12

2 tablespoons coconut oil
¼ cup maple syrup
1 teaspoon ground ginger
1 teaspoon curry powder
½ teaspoon cayenne
¼ teaspoon onion powder
¼ teaspoon garlic powder
3 cups shelled walnuts

1. Place coconut oil in a 2–4-quart slow cooker, turn on high, and allow oil to melt.

2. While oil is melting, mix maple syrup, ginger, curry powder, cayenne, onion powder, and garlic powder together in a small bowl.

3. Once oil has melted, add walnuts to slow cooker and stir. Add maple syrup mixture to slow cooker, and stir until nuts are evenly coated.

4. Cover and cook on high for 1 hour. Stir nuts, replace cover, and cook for another hour.

5. Remove cover and cook for an additional 20–30 minutes, until nuts are dry. Cool and store in airtight containers.

Sweet and Spicy Nut Mix

Nuts are a wonderful snack for any diet. They are full of fiber, healthy fats, and vitamins and minerals. And they are very satisfying. There is no way you'll eat this nut mix and be hungry again an hour later. Use your favorite nuts in this easy recipe and adjust the spice mixture to your taste.

INGREDIENTS | MAKES 6 CUPS

3 teaspoons Ener-G Egg Replacer mixed with 4 tablespoons water

1 teaspoon lemon juice

¼ teaspoon salt

2 tablespoons maple syrup

1½ teaspoons cinnamon

1 teaspoon chili powder

½ teaspoon cayenne pepper

½ cup finely chopped coconut

2 cups walnuts

2 cups pecans

2 cups hazelnuts

¼ cup extra-virgin olive oil

3 tablespoons coconut oil, melted

1. Preheat oven to 325°F. In large bowl, beat egg replacer mixture with lemon juice and salt until stiff peaks form. Beat in maple syrup, cinnamon, chili powder, and cayenne pepper until combined. Stir in coconut.

2. Fold in walnuts, pecans, and hazelnuts until nuts are coated.

3. Spread olive oil and coconut oil in 15" × 10" jellyroll pan. Spread nuts over oil mixture. Bake for 40 minutes, stirring every 10 minutes, until nuts are light golden brown and crisp and oil is absorbed. Let cool, then store in an airtight container at room temperature.

Peppered Almonds

Serve these at a cocktail party as an alternative to plain salted nuts. They are also delicious stirred into trail mix.

INGREDIENTS | MAKES 2½ CUPS

2½ cups skin-on almonds or mixed nuts

1 teaspoon olive oil

½ teaspoon ground jalapeño

½ teaspoon garlic powder

½ teaspoon cayenne pepper

½ teaspoon ground chipotle

½ teaspoon ground paprika

1. Place nuts in a 2–4-quart slow cooker. Drizzle with oil. Stir. Add remaining ingredients and stir again to distribute seasonings evenly.

2. Cover slow cooker and cook on low for 1 hour. Uncover and cook on low for 15 minutes or until nuts look dry.

Slow-Cooked Party Mix

Grab it while it's hot, because it won't last long once the guests arrive!

INGREDIENTS | SERVES 24

4 tablespoons olive oil
3 tablespoons lime juice
2 teaspoons garlic powder
2 teaspoons onion powder
1 cup raw almonds
1 cup raw pecans
1 cup raw walnut pieces
1 cup raw cashews
2 cups raw pumpkin seeds, shelled
1 cup raw sunflower seeds, shelled

1. Add oil to a 2-quart slow cooker. Then add lime juice, garlic powder, and onion powder, and stir all together.

2. Add remaining ingredients and stir well until nuts and seeds are evenly coated. Cover and cook on low for 5–6 hours, stirring occasionally.

3. Uncover slow cooker, stir, and cook for another 45–60 minutes, to dry nuts and seeds. Cool and store in airtight container.

Toasted Hazelnuts and Dates

Hazelnuts should be toasted on a baking sheet in a preheated, 350°F oven for 8–10 minutes before using.

INGREDIENTS | SERVES 8

2 cups pitted dates, soaked in water overnight

⅔ cup boiling water

½ cup maple syrup

Strips of peel from 1 lemon (yellow part only)

¼ cup toasted hazelnuts

1. Drain dates and place in a 4½-quart slow cooker.

2. Add boiling water, maple syrup, and lemon peel. Cover and cook on high for 3 hours.

3. Discard lemon peel. Place dates on a serving dish and sprinkle with hazelnuts.

"Butterscotch-Caramel" Glazed Nuts

These nuts taste even better when sprinkled over some Crustless Apple Pie (see recipe in Chapter 14).

INGREDIENTS | SERVES 32

4 cups raw almonds, pecan halves, or walnut halves

½ cup "Butterscotch-Caramel" Sauce (see recipe in Chapter 12)

1½ teaspoons cinnamon

1. Add all ingredients to a 1-quart slow cooker. Stir to coat nuts. Cover and cook on low for 3 hours, stirring at least once an hour.

2. Uncover slow cooker. Stirring mixture every 20 minutes, cook on low for 1 more hour, or until nuts are almost dry.

3. Line a baking sheet with parchment paper. Evenly spread nuts on the sheet and allow to cool completely. Store in a covered container.

Blueberry Trail Mix

This trail mix is the perfect blend of fruit, nuts, and seeds, and it's sure to cure those afternoon hunger pangs.

INGREDIENTS | SERVES 2

¼ cup dried blueberries

¼ cup pumpkin seeds

¼ cup almonds

¼ teaspoon cinnamon

Combine all ingredients in a medium bowl. Serve immediately or store in an airtight container.

Antioxidants

Antioxidants are important for attacking free radicals in your body. You really can't eat enough foods containing these important compounds. Feel free to mix up the type of berry you add to this mix. If you're going to serve the mix right away, you can even use fresh berries when they're in season.

Traditional Trail Mix

This trail mix has less sugar than conventional trail mixes. For a different flavor, vary the nuts, seeds, or dried fruits.

INGREDIENTS | SERVES 4

1 cup raw or roasted almonds
1 cup pumpkin seeds
½ cup sunflower seeds
1 cup dehydrated strawberries
½ cup goji berries

Combine all ingredients in a medium bowl. Serve immediately or store in an airtight container.

Pistachio-Pumpkin Trail Mix

This trail mix is sure to satisfy an active family on the go. Feel free to mix up the types of nuts or fruits you add in to make it your own personal trail mix.

INGREDIENTS | SERVES 4

½ cup pistachio nuts
½ cup pumpkin seeds
½ cup sunflower seeds
½ cup unsweetened coconut flakes
1 cup dried mulberries

Combine all ingredients in a medium bowl. Serve immediately or store in an airtight container.

Trail Mix Crunch

If you sometimes miss potato chips and other crunchy snacks, this is the trail mix for you. It has a sweet and salty taste to satisfy your cravings.

INGREDIENTS | SERVES 8

½ cup cashews
½ cup almonds
½ cup macadamia nuts
½ cup pistachio nuts
4 tablespoons maple syrup
1 teaspoon sea salt
½ teaspoon ground black pepper
¼ teaspoon ground cumin
1 teaspoon curry powder
Pinch ground cloves
1 teaspoon ground cinnamon

1. Preheat oven to 300°F.

2. Place cashews, almonds, macadamias, and pistachios on a large baking sheet and bake for 10–12 minutes, taking care they do not burn. Remove from oven and let cool approximately 5 minutes.

3. In a small bowl, mix maple syrup, salt, pepper, cumin, curry powder, cloves, and cinnamon.

4. In a large saucepan over medium heat, place nuts and half the maple syrup mixture. When mixture begins to melt, mix in remaining maple syrup mixture.

5. Shake the pan and stir until nuts are coated, about 5 minutes.

6. Remove nuts from the pan and spread them out on a sheet of parchment paper. Use a spoon to separate nuts that stick together. Let dry for about 30 minutes. Trail mix will keep for about a week in an airtight container.

CHAPTER 14

Desserts

Easy Banana Date Cookies

These cookies are simple and refined sugar–free.

INGREDIENTS | MAKES 12

1 cup chopped pitted dates
1 medium banana, peeled
¼ teaspoon vanilla
1¾ cups unsweetened coconut flakes

1. Preheat oven to 375°F. Cover dates in water and soak for about 10 minutes until softened. Drain.

2. Process together dates, banana, and vanilla until almost smooth. Stir in coconut flakes by hand until thick. You may need a little more or less than 1¾ cups.

3. Drop by generous tablespoonfuls onto a cookie sheet. Bake 10–12 minutes or until golden brown. Cookies will be soft and chewy.

Chocolate "Graham" Cracker Bars

It's nice to have a sweet treat every once in a while. Just make sure that the sweets you eat are high quality and very delicious. Look for dark chocolate with a high percentage of cacao. Then enjoy every bite.

INGREDIENTS | SERVES 8

1 cup finely chopped walnuts

1 cup unsweetened grated coconut

3 cups crushed "Graham" Crackers (see recipe in Chapter 8)

⅔ cup coconut milk

14 ounces chopped dark chocolate

2 teaspoons vanilla

1. Grease a 9" square pan with coconut oil and set aside. In a large bowl, combine walnuts, coconut, and cracker crumbs; set aside.

2. In saucepan, combine coconut milk and chocolate. Melt over low heat, stirring frequently, until smooth. Stir in vanilla. Reserve ⅓ cup of this mixture.

3. Pour remaining chocolate mixture over crumb mixture and stir to coat.

4. Press crumb mixture into prepared pan and spread reserved chocolate over top. Place in refrigerator until set; cut into small squares to serve.

Heavenly Cookie Bars

These cookie bars are amazing!
Dates add sweetness and chewiness to this healthy dessert.

INGREDIENTS | MAKES 48

2 cups maple syrup
4 cups almond flour
½ teaspoon nutmeg
½ teaspoon ginger
½ cup dates, chopped
2 cups ground walnuts
½ cup raisins

1. Preheat oven to 350°F. Line 2 baking sheets with parchment paper.

2. Warm maple syrup in a saucepan over low heat for 5 minutes and let cool slightly.

3. In a medium bowl, sift together flour, nutmeg, and ginger. Add maple syrup and stir until well blended. Stir in dates, walnuts, and raisins.

4. Roll dough to ¼" thick and cut into squares. Place squares on prepared baking sheets and bake for 10 minutes. Remove to rack to cool.

Frozen Chocolate Coconut Milk Treats

These coconut milk squares are not as creamy as ice cream but are a nice alternative. You can change the flavor by changing the fruit purée that you add into the recipe.

INGREDIENTS | SERVES 10

12 tablespoons raw cacao powder

6 tablespoons fresh fruit purée of your choice

6 tablespoons coconut oil

6 tablespoons coconut milk

3 tablespoons unsweetened shredded coconut

2 tablespoons cacao nibs

1 ripe banana

1. Combine all ingredients in food processor and pulse until very smooth. Add water if the consistency is not fluid.

2. Pour into ice cube trays and freeze for at least 6 hours.

Coconut

Coconut has many great properties. This recipe uses all the edible parts of the coconut—the meat, oil, and milk. You will receive high fiber, vitamin, and mineral content as well as skin benefits from consumption of coconut.

Walnut-Stuffed Slow-Cooked Apples

Walnuts are an excellent source of omega-3s, vitamin E, and a variety of other phytonutrients and antioxidants.

INGREDIENTS | SERVES 4

¼ cup coarsely chopped walnuts

3 tablespoons dried currants

¾ teaspoon ground cinnamon, divided

4 medium Granny Smith apples, cored

1 cup maple syrup

¾ cup apple cider

1. In a small bowl, combine walnuts and currants. Add ¼ teaspoon cinnamon, stirring to combine.

2. Place apples in a 2-quart or smaller slow cooker. Spoon walnut mixture into the cavity of each apple.

3. In a mixing bowl, combine remaining ½ teaspoon cinnamon, maple syrup, and apple cider, stirring to combine. Pour over apples in the slow cooker.

4. Cover and cook on low for 2¾ hours. Remove apples with a slotted spoon.

5. Spoon ¼ cup cooking liquid over each serving.

Baked Bananas

This healthy dessert is sure to be a favorite of yours. Make it in bulk and use to spread on Paleo Sandwich Bread (see recipe in Chapter 3) or Soft Breakfast Bread (see recipe in Chapter 2).

INGREDIENTS | SERVES 4

4 small bananas, peeled
½ teaspoon grated orange rind
½ tablespoon fruit purée
1 tablespoon lemon juice
⅛ teaspoon cinnamon
⅛ teaspoon nutmeg
1 tablespoon coconut oil, melted
1 tablespoon cacao nibs

1. Preheat oven to 350°F.

2. Cut each banana lengthwise and across into 8 pieces. Arrange banana slices in a small baking pan.

3. Sprinkle evenly with orange rind, fruit purée, lemon juice, cinnamon, nutmeg, and coconut oil.

4. Bake uncovered for 35–40 minutes, basting after 15 minutes with liquid in baking pan.

5. Sprinkle with cacao nibs before serving.

Mixed-Fruit Mini Pies

Mixing fruit is a great way to give pies more flavor, but you must choose fruit that cooks in about the same time so all of them will be tender and sweet. Delicate fruits such as peaches, raspberries, and blueberries will become tender at the same time. When topped with a sweet and crunchy mixture, these individual pies are irresistible.

INGREDIENTS | SERVES 6

½ cup coconut flour

¼ cup hazelnut or almond flour

½ cup chopped toasted hazelnuts or almonds

¼ cup shredded coconut

⅓ cup coconut oil, melted

2 tablespoons maple syrup, divided

¼ teaspoon salt

3 ripe peaches, peeled and chopped

1 cup blueberries

1 cup raspberries

1 teaspoon vanilla

1 tablespoon orange juice

1. Preheat oven to 400°F. Grease 6 (1-cup) ovenproof custard cups with coconut oil and set aside.

2. In medium bowl, combine coconut flour, hazelnut flour, hazelnuts, and coconut and toss. Add melted coconut oil, 1 tablespoon maple syrup, and salt and mix until crumbly; set aside.

3. In medium bowl, combine peaches, blueberries, and raspberries. Sprinkle with vanilla, orange juice, and remaining 1 tablespoon maple syrup and toss gently. Divide among prepared custard cups. Top with crumble mixture.

4. Place custard cups on a rimmed baking sheet and bake for 20–30 minutes or until fruit is bubbly and tender and topping is browned. Serve warm or cool.

Crustless Apple Pie

Adjust the cooking time depending on the type of apple you use. A softer Golden Delicious should be cooked through and soft in the recommended cooking times, but a crisper Granny Smith apple may take longer.

INGREDIENTS | SERVES 8

8 medium apples, peeled, cored, and sliced

3 tablespoons orange juice

3 tablespoons water

½ cup chopped pecans

⅓ cup maple syrup

¼ cup coconut butter, melted

½ teaspoon cinnamon

1. Grease a 4½-quart slow cooker with olive oil. Arrange apple slices to cover the bottom of the slow cooker.

2. In a small bowl or measuring cup, stir orange juice and water to mix. Evenly drizzle over apples.

3. In another small bowl, combine pecans, maple syrup, coconut butter, and cinnamon; mix well. Evenly crumble pecan mixture over apples.

4. Cover and cook on high for 2 hours or on low for 4 hours. Serve warm or chilled.

Apple-Date "Crisp"

*Golden Delicious apples are suggested here, but go ahead and
try a different type of baking apple of your choice.*

INGREDIENTS | SERVES 6

6 cups cored, peeled, and thinly sliced
Golden Delicious apples

2 teaspoons lemon juice

⅓ cup chopped dates

1⅓ cups finely chopped almonds

½ cup almond flour

½ cup maple syrup

½ teaspoon ground cinnamon

½ teaspoon ground ginger

⅛ teaspoon ground nutmeg

⅛ teaspoon ground cloves

4 tablespoons coconut butter

1. Combine apples, lemon juice, and dates in a bowl, and
   mix well. Transfer mixture to a 4½-quart slow cooker.

2. In a separate bowl, combine almonds, flour, maple
   syrup, cinnamon, ginger, nutmeg, and cloves. Cut in
   coconut butter with 2 knives or a pastry blender.
   Sprinkle nut mixture over apples and smooth down.

3. Cook on low for 4 hours. Serve warm.

Crisp Variations

Experiment with a variety of crisp ingredients like walnuts and pecans. Try using
coconut oil instead of coconut butter.

Peach Cobbler

*Cobbler is a versatile sweet dish that can be enjoyed as a warm
and tasty eye opener or as a postdinner dessert.*

INGREDIENTS | SERVES 8

2 (16-ounce) packages frozen peaches,
thawed and drained

¾ cup plus 1 tablespoon maple
syrup, divided

2 teaspoons ground cinnamon, divided

½ teaspoon ground nutmeg

¾ cup almond flour

6 tablespoons coconut butter

1. Combine peaches, ¾ cup maple syrup, 1½ teaspoons cinnamon, and nutmeg in a large bowl. Transfer to a 4½-quart slow cooker.

2. In a separate bowl, combine flour with 1 tablespoon remaining maple syrup and ½ teaspoon cinnamon.

3. Cut in coconut butter with 2 knives or a pastry blender and then spread mixture over peaches.

4. Cover and cook on high for 2 hours. Serve warm.

Blueberry Coconut Crisp

Among their many virtues, blueberries are low on the glycemic index, in spite of their inherent sweetness. Taste the berries before you make this recipe. You may find you don't need a sweetener at all.

INGREDIENTS | SERVES 6–8

4 cups fresh blueberries

¼ cup maple syrup, if needed

1½ teaspoons vanilla

1 tablespoon lemon juice

1 cup chopped pecans

1 cup unsweetened shredded coconut

⅓ cup coconut flour

6 tablespoons coconut oil

⅛ teaspoon salt

1. Preheat oven to 400°F. Grease an 8" square glass pan with coconut oil.

2. Combine blueberries, maple syrup (if using), vanilla, and lemon juice in the pan and toss gently; set aside.

3. In medium bowl, combine pecans, coconut, and coconut flour. Add coconut oil and salt and mix until crumbly. Sprinkle over blueberries.

4. Bake for 35–40 minutes or until blueberry mixture is bubbly. Serve warm or cool.

Plum Blueberry Coconut Crumble

Plums are in season in summer and early fall. These sweet stone fruits have a low glycemic index rating and are low in carbohydrates and rich in vitamins A and C. Serve this crumble warm from the oven.

INGREDIENTS | SERVES 4

8 medium plums, stones removed, sliced
2 cups blueberries
2 tablespoons maple syrup
2 tablespoons lemon juice
1 tablespoon arrowroot powder
2 cups unsweetened coconut flakes
1 cup chopped pecans
⅔ cup coconut flour
¼ teaspoon baking soda
½ teaspoon cream of tartar
¼ teaspoon salt
⅓ cup coconut oil, melted

1. Preheat oven to 350°F. Grease a 9" square baking dish with coconut oil.

2. Combine plums and blueberries in prepared dish. Drizzle with maple syrup, lemon juice, and arrowroot powder and toss to coat.

3. In medium bowl, combine coconut flakes, pecans, coconut flour, baking soda, cream of tartar, and salt. Add coconut oil and mix until crumbly. Pat mixture on top of fruit in dish.

4. Bake for 40–45 minutes or until fruit is bubbly and topping is golden. Serve warm.

Coconut Drops

This recipe couldn't be simpler or more delicious. With just two ingredients, you do need to buy the best chocolate and the best and freshest coconut you can find. Holding some of the chocolate back and adding it to the rest after it has melted and been removed from the heat will "temper" the chocolate so it will stay solid at room temperature.

INGREDIENTS | MAKES 2 POUNDS

1½ pounds dark chocolate, chopped
2½ cups unsweetened shredded coconut

1. In heavy saucepan, melt all but ½ cup chocolate over low heat, stirring frequently, until melted and smooth.

2. Remove pan from heat and stir in reserved chocolate. Stir constantly until mixture is smooth again.

3. Add coconut and mix well.

4. Drop mounds of this mixture onto parchment paper. Let stand until set. Store in airtight container at room temperature.

Cranberry-Apple Compote

This compote is an easy, succulent taste of fall.

INGREDIENTS | SERVES 6

4 cups peeled, cored, sliced apples
½ cup sliced cranberries
⅓ cup maple syrup
2 tablespoons coconut oil
1 teaspoon ground cinnamon
¼ teaspoon ground nutmeg
¾ cup combined chopped walnuts and almonds

1. Combine all ingredients except nuts in a 3–4-quart slow cooker.

2. Cover and cook on high for 1½–2 hours or until apples are tender.

3. Sprinkle each serving with nuts.

Bananas Foster

Bananas Foster is not just good . . . it's heavenly. It's the perfect dessert for the Vegan Paleo diet.

INGREDIENTS | SERVES 3

3 large overripe bananas, peeled
4 tablespoons coconut butter
⅓ cup maple syrup
1 teaspoon vanilla extract

1. In a medium bowl, mash bananas with a fork or potato masher. Transfer mashed bananas to a 2-quart slow cooker. Add coconut butter, maple syrup, and vanilla.

2. Cover and cook on low for 3–4 hours or on high for 1–2 hours.

Vanilla-Infused Fruit Cocktail

Try this recipe with a different fruit combination each time.

INGREDIENTS | SERVES 8

16 ounces prunes, pitted
8 ounces dried apricots
8 ounces dried pears
3 cups water
½ cup maple syrup
2 tablespoons fresh lemon juice
1 teaspoon finely grated lemon zest
½ vanilla bean or ½ teaspoon vanilla

1. Combine all ingredients together in a 4–6-quart slow cooker.

2. Cook on low for about 6–8 hours or until fruit is tender.

3. Serve warm or at room temperature.

Spiced Poached Pears

The attractive finished product makes for a great holiday dish.

INGREDIENTS | SERVES 8

8 firm, ripe pears, peeled
½ cup sliced cranberries
¾ cup maple syrup
¼ teaspoon ground ginger
¼ teaspoon ground cinnamon
⅛ teaspoon ground cloves
Juice of 1 lemon
2 tablespoons lime juice

1. Stand pears upright in a 6-quart slow cooker. Sprinkle with cranberries.

2. In a small bowl, combine maple syrup, ginger, cinnamon, and cloves, and spoon on top of pears. Pour lemon and lime juice evenly over pears.

3. Cover and cook on low for 4 hours or on high for 2 hours.

Chunky Apple-Cherry Sauce

Enjoy warm as a breakfast fruit or chilled as a sweet summer treat.

INGREDIENTS | SERVES 6

5 large Golden Delicious apples, peeled, cored, and sliced

2 tablespoons water

¼ cup maple syrup

½ cup cherry purée

1. Place apple slices in a 4–6-quart slow cooker greased with coconut oil. Add water and maple syrup and toss to coat apples. Cover and cook on low for 6–7 hours.

2. Stir in cherry purée. Serve warm or allow to cool and serve chilled.

Paleo Chocolate Bars

These chocolate bars are quick to whip up and quick to eat. The amount of maple syrup can be varied depending on your desired sweetness level.

INGREDIENTS | SERVES 8

1 tablespoon maple syrup

4 tablespoons coconut oil

¼ cup ground almonds

¼ cup ground hazelnuts

¼ cup sunflower seeds

¼ cup cacao powder

¾ cup unsweetened coconut flakes

1. Melt maple syrup and coconut oil in saucepan over medium heat.

2. In a mixing bowl, combine almonds, hazelnuts, sunflower seeds, cacao powder, and coconut. Mix thoroughly. Add maple syrup mixture to bowl and mix well.

3. Pour dough into an 8" × 8" greased baking pan and refrigerate or freeze until firm, about 10 minutes.

4. Cut into squares and serve immediately or store in refrigerator.

Strawberry Coconut Ice Cream

Rich and creamy, this is the most decadent dairy-free strawberry ice cream you'll ever taste.

INGREDIENTS | SERVES 6

2 cups coconut cream
1¾ cups frozen strawberries
¾ cup coconut sugar
2 teaspoons vanilla
¼ teaspoon salt

1. Combine all ingredients in a food processor or blender. Purée until smooth and creamy.

2. Transfer mixture to a large freezer-proof baking or casserole dish and place in freezer.

3. Stir mixture every 30 minutes until a smooth ice cream forms, about 4 hours. If mixture gets too firm to stir, transfer to a blender, process until smooth, then return to freezer.

Apricot Ginger Sorbet

Made with real fruit and without dairy, this is a nearly fat-free treat that you can add to smoothies or just enjoy outside on a hot summer day.

INGREDIENTS | SERVES 6

⅔ cup water
⅔ cup maple syrup
2 teaspoons minced fresh ginger
5 cups chopped apricots, fresh or frozen
3 tablespoons lemon juice

1. In a small saucepan over medium-high heat, bring water, maple syrup, and ginger to a boil, then reduce heat to low. Simmer for 3–4 minutes until a syrup forms. Allow to cool.

2. Combine maple syrup mixture, apricots, and lemon juice in a food processor or blender. Purée until smooth.

3. Transfer mixture to a large freezer-proof baking or casserole dish and place in freezer.

4. Stir mixture every 30 minutes until frozen and smooth, about 4 hours. If mixture gets too firm, transfer to a blender, process until smooth, then return to freezer.

Mango "Creamsicle" Sorbet

When the weather is hot and you're looking for a cold, refreshing treat, try this homemade sorbet recipe.

INGREDIENTS | SERVES 6

3 cups chopped peeled mangoes
or peaches
½ cup cold water
1 cup unsweetened shredded coconut
2 tablespoons lemon juice

1. In a food processor or blender, combine mangoes and water; process until smooth. Add coconut and lemon juice; process until smooth.

2. Transfer to a plastic container and freeze until solid, about 2 hours.

Sorbet

Try this recipe with other favorite fruits. If the sorbet does not seem sweet enough, add maple syrup to the mixture next time. There is none added here because mango has a high sugar content on its own.

Watermelon Raspberry Granita

Watermelon is a great source of lycopene, an antioxidant that helps protect against cell damage. It's also an excellent source of vitamin C and potassium. Plus, it's delicious and naturally sweet. A granita is a bit different from a sherbet or sorbet. The fruit mixture is scraped with a fork several times while freezing so it has a beautiful crystalline structure.

INGREDIENTS | SERVES 4

4 cups chopped watermelon
1 cup raspberries
¼ cup maple syrup
2 tablespoons lemon juice
Pinch salt

1. In two batches, combine watermelon, raspberries, maple syrup, lemon juice, and salt in a blender or food processor. Blend or process until smooth.

2. Pour mixture into a 9" square baking dish. Freeze for 3 hours, then remove from freezer and use a fork to scrape mixture into small pieces, paying special attention to the sides of the baking dish. Return to freezer and freeze for another hour.

3. Scrape mixture again with a fork. Serve immediately, or spoon lightly into a bowl and freeze, covered, for up to 2 days. Scrape with a fork into serving dish and eat immediately.

Appendix A:
Vegan Paleo "Yes" Foods

In order to ensure your success on the Vegan Paleo diet, you need to stock your pantry with fresh, organic produce, fruits, seeds, nuts, etc. This list contains both the basics and the obscure. Feel free to experiment with items you would not normally choose. That will spice things up and keep you interested in the diet.

apple	collard greens	nectarine
apricot	cranberries (regular	onion
artichoke	and dried)	orange
arugula	cucumber	papaya
asparagus	dandelion	passion fruit
avocado	eggplant	peach
banana	endive	pear
beet greens	fiddlehead	persimmon
bell pepper	figs	pineapple
bitterleaf	Florence fennel	plum
blackberries	flowers and flower buds	pomegranate
blueberries	garlic	radicchio
bok choy	grapefruit	raspberries
broccoli	grapes	rhubarb
broccoli rabe	guava	spinach
Brussels sprouts	honeydew melon	squash
bulb and stem vegetables	kale	sweet pepper
cabbage	kiwi	Swiss chard
cantaloupe	kohlrabi	tomatillo
cauliflower	leek	tomato
celery	lemon	turnip
cherries	lettuce	watercress
chicory	lime	yarrow
Chinese cabbage	mandarin orange	zucchini
coconut	mango	

Appendix B:
Foods to Avoid

The following is a list of foods you should avoid. Remember, if anything is meat or animal based, it doesn't work with the Vegan Paleo diet.

alligator
bass
bear
beef
bison
bluefish
caribou
cheese
chicken breast
chuck steak
clams
cod
crab
crayfish
dairy milk
egg whites
eggs
flank steak
game hen breasts

goat
grouper
haddock
halibut
hamburger
herring
honey
liver (beef, lamb, goat,
    or chicken)
lobster
London broil
mackerel
marrow (beef, lamb,
    or goat)
mussels
orange roughy
ostrich
oysters
pheasant

pork
quail
rabbit
rattlesnake
red snapper
salmon
scallops
scrod
shrimp
tilapia
tongue (beef, lamb,
    or goat)
trout
tuna
turkey
veal
venison

Index